USAF

The BATs
The History of Iowa's Air National Guard
174th Squadron—From Fighter to Tanker

The boldest statement of the 174th Bats was displayed for all to see on the vertical stabilizers of their F-16s. (*185th FW/McCallum collection*)

Garry R. Pape

Schiffer Publishing Ltd
4880 Lower Valley Road • Atglen, PA 19310

Dedication

In the mid-1950s, twin brothers William M. and James H. Belote were working towards their Doctorates at the University of California Berkeley and became regular members at my family's home; Bill would eventually marry my sister, Marilyn. History majors and very interested in aviation, they served overseas in the U.S. Army Air Forces during World War II. It is all their fault that I became so interested in aviation history. This book is a product of that interest.

Library of Congress Control Number: 2013954743

Printed in China.
ISBN: 978-0-7643-4374-2

We are interested in hearing from authors with book ideas on related topics.

Published by Schiffer Publishing Ltd.
4880 Lower Valley Road
Atglen, PA 19310
Phone: (610) 593-1777
FAX: (610) 593-2002
E-mail: Info@schifferbooks.com.
Visit our web site at: www.schifferbooks.com
Please write for a free catalog.
This book may be purchased
from the publisher.
Try your bookstore first.

Contents

Acknowledgments

When my wife and I moved to Iowa from southern California in early 2004, I wondered if I could find anyone interested in aviation history. We weren't here long and I met Duane E. "Mac" McCallum. Mac had a long history with the 174th Fighter Squadron and the subsequent 185th Fighter Group. The 174th Fighter Squadron, Single Engine was recognized on December 2, 1946. Mac joined the squadron in October 1947, and went to Bangor, Maine, when the squadron was mobilized for the Korean War. During those years he worked first as an airplane mechanic and then supply. When the squadron was relieved from active duty in December 1952, Mac returned to Sioux City and did not reenlist in the guard. After a few months he did rejoin. In 1954, Mac requested to go to photography school. From 1954 until he retired in 1985, he was the head of photo services and had reached the rank of Master Sergeant.

There was another gentleman who did a lot for the 174th Fighter Squadron history: Robert F. "Bob" Stolze. Bob joined the 174th Fighter Squadron in early 1947 and was an aircraft mechanic. He too went to Bangor, Maine, in 1951, but when the squadron was returned to state control in December, Bob retired at the rank of Master Sergeant. What Bob did while in the squadron was a lot for squadron history. As the squadron did not have an official photographer for all the years he was part of it, he took all the photos that we have for the 1947 through 1953 period. It is said of Bob Stolze that "he always had a camera around his neck."

MSgt. Duane E. "Mac" McCallum.

Bob Stolze and Mac McCallum became good friends, and both Bob's photos and information were passed on to Mac. When Bob passed away some years ago, his relatives gave Mac Bob's 174th Fighter Squadron collection. Over the years Mac has built his own collection, to the point that he has thousands of photos, negatives, and slides covering the 174th Fighter Squadron/185th Fighter Group (later Wing) through most of the 1990s. Mac's

Robert F. Stolze.

collection also included squadron scrap books covering the decades and copies of newsletters put out by the Sioux City Air Guard, as well as 40th, 50th, and 60th anniversary books put out by the 185th.

Assistance was provided very generously by a number of people and organizations: Grace E. Linden and Thomas Munson, Curators of History, Sioux City Public Museum; David P. Anderson, Senior Historian, ANG History Office, NGB/HO; the staff at the Sioux City Public Library and the use of their microfilm newspaper files; Lawrence G. Harrington and the RATs (Retired Air Technicians); and Master Sgt. William R. Wiseman, 185th Air Refueling Wing historian. Most of the photos concerning tanker operations are from the 185th ARW website.

A number of past 174th troops have been very helpful in allowing me to interview them with my trusty tape recorder (I'm old school), and/or answered questions via mail or e-mail: Roger L. Benson, Robert C. Eybers, Gary G. Grasma, Jon P. Haddock, Darrell E. Lake, Duane E. "Mac" McCallum, Warren G. "Bud" Nelson, Patrick C. Parks, and Lloyd A. Pippett.

Introduction

A Uniquely American Concept

The citizen-soldier of today is greatly respected. Whether Air or Army National Guard, they are responsible for a greater part of the national defense than they have shouldered for most of their existence.

Before the United States of America became an independent nation, the first citizen-soldier organizations were found in several settlements of the Massachusetts Bay Colony for local defense. In 1636, these units were combined into a formal military organization.

As time went on, other colonies formed local militias, all made up of local butchers, bakers, and candlestick makers. They fought with the King's Regulars in several wars between the late seventeenth century and through the greater part of the eighteenth century, up to 1775.

The Minutemen of the Revolution were the early National Guardsmen of the U.S. (*Library of Congress*)

On April 19, 1775, the "shot heard around the world" was fired by a group of militiamen known as the Minutemen (show up for duty within a minute). Throughout the war for independence, led by a militiaman named George Washington, the United States of America was established and the national history of a national militia was inaugurated.

With independence won, as happens at the end of many wars, there was a drawdown of the military. Matter of fact, it was disbanded, and thought that no military was needed. By 1792, the need for a military was reconsidered and the Federal Militia Act of that year was issued, which established the need for such an organization.

These militias were called to active duty several times during the nineteenth century. Most notable of these call-ups was the War of 1812, the war with Mexico, the American Civil War, and the Spanish-American War.

Aviation in the Army

Ballooning activities started in the United States in the late eighteenth century and flourished during the first half of the nineteenth century. The aeronauts (balloonists) that performed all across the country were referred to as Professors (showmen rather than educators).

By the time the American Civil War began in 1861, the U.S. Army had shown very little interest in the balloon as an instrument of warfare. But a number of civilian aeronauts were convinced that the balloon should be part of the army's arsenal and

Civilian balloonists, commonly called aeronauts, put pressure on the Army to incorporate aerial operations in the U.S. Civil War. (*Library of Congress*)

lobbied hard to get the army to use their services and balloons.

Primary among the aeronauts were James Allen, John La Mountain, Thaddeus S. C. Lowe, and John Wise. The most successful was Lowe, who garnered the title Chief Aeronaut (though no military rank). Their success was mixed. Lack of interest and/or understanding on the army's part, and egotism and internal struggles among the aeronauts contributed to a lack of greater success.

After the Civil War, the army was greatly reduced. Balloons were of minor interest to the army, as they were busy protecting wagon trains across the American West and fighting Indian wars.

In 1891, the U.S. Army established its Signal Corps, and the first Chief Signal Officer was Brigadier General Adolphus W. Greely (who had started his military career in the 19th Massachusetts Infantry). Under Greely, aeronautic facilities were established and ballooning had a supporter.

Limited ballooning activities were carried out during the last decade of the nineteenth century. In the Spanish-American War, an observation balloon was used during the Battle of San Juan Hill in Cuba.

Professor Thaddeus Lower was the most prominent of the balloonists in the Civil War. The Army had their doubts about the balloons and gave little support. (*Library of Congress*)

By the turn of the twentieth century, the major European powers were investing in steerable balloons (dirigibles). The United States Army would not have their first dirigible for nearly a decade, and a relatively small one at that.

On a cold and windy day in mid-December 1903, Orville and Wilbur Wright made aviation history over the sands of Kitty Hawk, North Carolina. The first powered flying machine took to the air, and human history would be changed forever.

Over the next five years, the Wright brothers would refine their design. Within a year from their inaugural powered flight, they started to get letters from foreign governments professing interest in their invention. Soon they were performing demonstration flights in Europe. But the U.S. Army showed little

The use of balloons in the U.S. Army dwindled away until the Spanish-American War, when its use was put into action again, this time in Cuba. (*Library of Congress*)

The Wrights, with their Military Flyer at Fort Myer, Virginia, in 1909. Apparently Wilbur Wright, on the left, was not thrilled about having his picture taken. (*Library of Congress*)

interest. There was good reason for this resistance to investigate the Wright's new flying machine. They (along with the Smithsonian Institution) had invested funds in the powered flying machine of Samuel P. Langley in the late 1890s. Langley made a number of unsuccessful attempts at powered flight, one nine days prior to the Wrights' successful initial powered flight. The army decided not to invest any further funds in the Langley experiment, and for a number of years were skeptical about the Wrights' flying machine.

In 1907, the U.S. Army started to consider a powered flying machine. Within time a specification was developed, bids received and evaluated, and a September flyoff was to take place at Fort Myer, Virginia, between the Wright Military Flyer and an aeroplane designed by Augustus M. Herring. Herring defaulted; his design was not ready. The Wrights' flew, and military aviation in the U.S. was born.

National Guard Goes Atmospheric

As the army was preparing for powered flight trials in 1908, the 71st Regiment of New York's National Guard was planning to take flight. Major Oscar Erlandean, commander of First Company, Signal Corps, along with the 100 men of his company attended their first lesson in ballooning April 30, 1908. From this Major Erlandean organized an "aeronautic corps" of 25 men.

The Wright Military Flyer during its demonstration flight over Fort Myer. (*Library of Congress*)

The BATs The History of Iowa's Air National Guard 174th Squadron—From Fighter to Tanker

Charles A. Lindbergh, on the right, was also a supporter of aviation in the National Guard. Lindbergh was a member of Missouri's 110th Observation Squadron. (*Library of Congress*)

The United States entered World War I on April 6, 1917. Soon after, the War Department declared that all National Guard units would be disbanded. On May 23, 1917, the First Aero Company was disbanded.

Postwar Air Units

On November 11, 1918, World War I was over. Aviation — military aviation especially — would never be the same. Aeronautical design and military tactics had changed drastically. National Guardsmen serving in active duty units made a proud record for themselves and reflected greatly on their prior Guard units.

In September 1919, the Militia Bureau, which oversaw Guard activity, asked Major General Charles T. Menoher, Chief of the Army Air Service, about how the National Guard air units would fit into Air Service plans. General Menoher replied that such air organizations had no place in Air Service planning.

Menoher was overruled, and on February 10, 1920, the War Department authorized an air unit for each National Guard infantry division. Between 1921 and 1941, 29 National Guard observation squadrons received federal recognition. Among these squadrons was Missouri's 110th Observation Squadron, which had Captain Charles A. Lindbergh on its roster.

The use of balloons in the U.S. Army dwindled away until the Spanish-American War, when its use was put into action again, this time in Cuba. (*Library of Congress*)

interest. There was good reason for this resistance to investigate the Wright's new flying machine. They (along with the Smithsonian Institution) had invested funds in the powered flying machine of Samuel P. Langley in the late 1890s. Langley made a number of unsuccessful attempts at powered flight, one nine days prior to the Wrights' successful initial powered flight. The army decided not to invest any further funds in the Langley experiment, and for a number of years were skeptical about the Wrights' flying machine.

In 1907, the U.S. Army started to consider a powered flying machine. Within time a specification was developed, bids received and evaluated, and a September flyoff was to take place at Fort Myer, Virginia, between the Wright Military Flyer and an aeroplane designed by Augustus M. Herring. Herring defaulted; his design was not ready. The Wrights' flew, and military aviation in the U.S. was born.

The Wrights, with their Military Flyer at Fort Myer, Virginia, in 1909. Apparently Wilbur Wright, on the left, was not thrilled about having his picture taken. (*Library of Congress*)

National Guard Goes Atmospheric

As the army was preparing for powered flight trials in 1908, the 71st Regiment of New York's National Guard was planning to take flight. Major Oscar Erlandean, commander of First Company, Signal Corps, along with the 100 men of his company attended their first lesson in ballooning April 30, 1908. From this Major Erlandean organized an "aeronautic corps" of 25 men.

The Wright Military Flyer during its demonstration flight over Fort Myer. (*Library of Congress*)

A. M. Herring, C. M. Manly, A. R. Hawley, and J. A. D. McCuroy with their June Bug flying machine of the Aerial Experiment Association. (*Library of Congress*)

Between 1st Company's 1908 "class" and America entering the First World War on April 6, 1917, a number of state National Guard units attempted to establish flying units. New York's 1st Company and a Missouri company attempted ballooning, but neither apparently achieved flight. Powered flight was attempted by a number of state Guards, but none were as successful as New York's 1st Aero Company.

On November 1, 1915, the 1st Aero Company was organized. Captain Raynal C. Bolling (Bolling AFB is named after him) was in command. 1st Aero Company was mobilized July 13, 1916, as part of the conflict on the Mexican border against Pancho Villa. The Company trained at Mineola, New York. It was not sent to the border, and was released from federal service November 2, 1916.

General Billy Mitchell was a supporter of aviation in the National Guard. In this painting of the National Guard Bureau's Heritage Series, Mitchell is shown at Mineola, New York, in November 1916. A number of Army and National Guard aerial maneuvers took place there in the early twentieth century. (*National Guard Bureau/History Office*)

Lt. Thomas Selfridge and Alexander Graham Bell are shown strolling together. Selfridge took part in Bell's Aeronautical Experiment Association, which designed and flew early aeroplanes. From this association, Selfridge became the first U.S. Army officer to be an aircraft designer and the first pilot. Unfortunately, he also became a casualty when participating in the evaluation of the Wright Military Flyer. (*Air Force Historical Research Agency*)

Lt. Lahm, along with fellow Army balloonist Captain Charles de Forest Chandler, participated in ballooning events, such as this 1907 flight from St. Louis, Missouri, to Walton, West Virginia. (*Air Force Historical Research Agency*)

Lt. Frank P. Lahm and Lt. Benjamin D. Foulois were early advocates in Army aviation. They supported New York's National Guard's early struggle to incorporate aviation. (*Air Force Historical Research Agency*)

Charles A. Lindbergh, on the right, was also a supporter of aviation in the National Guard. Lindbergh was a member of Missouri's 110th Observation Squadron. (*Library of Congress*)

The United States entered World War I on April 6, 1917. Soon after, the War Department declared that all National Guard units would be disbanded. On May 23, 1917, the First Aero Company was disbanded.

Postwar Air Units

On November 11, 1918, World War I was over. Aviation — military aviation especially — would never be the same. Aeronautical design and military tactics had changed drastically. National Guardsmen serving in active duty units made a proud record for themselves and reflected greatly on their prior Guard units.

In September 1919, the Militia Bureau, which oversaw Guard activity, asked Major General Charles T. Menoher, Chief of the Army Air Service, about how the National Guard air units would fit into Air Service plans. General Menoher replied that such air organizations had no place in Air Service planning.

Menoher was overruled, and on February 10, 1920, the War Department authorized an air unit for each National Guard infantry division. Between 1921 and 1941, 29 National Guard observation squadrons received federal recognition. Among these squadrons was Missouri's 110th Observation Squadron, which had Captain Charles A. Lindbergh on its roster.

Iowa National Guard Observation Squadron

A group of pilots that had served during World War I attempted to get one of the new National Guard observation squadrons authorized for Iowa in 1925. No reason for the rejection of the request has been found. Apparently, five more attempts were made and rejected.

Perhaps with war clouds on the horizon, the National Guard Bureau contacted then-Iowa Governor George Wilson and Iowa's Adjutant

Royal C. Bolling. (*Library of Congress*)

Orville Wright, on the left, and Augustus Post of the Aero Club of America on the right. Post aided the New York National Guard in forming its aero unit in 1908. (*Air Force Historical Research Agency*)

1st Aero Company of the New York National Guard. (*National Guard Bureau/History Office*)

General, Charles H. Grahl, on May 15, 1940, and asked if Iowa was still interested in an air squadron. Their reply came in the affirmative five days later, and they stated the squadron would be stationed at the Des Moines Municipal Airport.

On July 30th of that year, the 124th Observation Squadron was allotted to the Iowa National Guard. During the rest of the year, money was obtained from the Works Progress Administration and the National Guard Bureau, along with private funds raised locally for the construction of a hangar and armory.

Recruiting was started when Major Lester G. Orcutt was appointed commanding officer. By late February, Major Orcutt had 300 applications, from which he picked 30 officers and 116 enlisted men. The squadron was activated February 25, 1941. The first aircraft, a North American BC-1 trainer, arrived March 9th. In April, their operational aircraft, Douglas O-38 and North American O-47 observation airplanes, were arriving. Major Orcutt checked out each of his new pilots, and by May they were flying their aircraft night and day.

The 124th Observation Squadron had to become proficient fast. On September 15, 1941, they were called to federal duty as part of the pre-war call up of all 29 National Guard observation squadrons. They were soon on their way to Sherman Army Air Field, near Leavenworth, Kansas. Until the 124th was disbanded on May 1, 1944, they were stationed in Texas, Louisiana, Tennessee, and Mississippi. They flew a variety of observation aircraft between 1941 and 1943, and flew P-38s, P-40s, and P-51s from 1943 on as a reconnaissance squadron (fighter) and tactical reconnaissance squadron.

North American Aviation, Inc. O-47A, similar to the ones flown by Iowa National Guard's 24th Observation Squadron. (*NASA-Ames Research Center Image Library*)

When the U.S. initially entered World War I, all National Guard flying units were disbanded, and individual guardsmen in the aviation units joined the U.S. Army's Air Service. In this war all Guard aviation squadrons were called to active duty and were integrated in the Army Air Forces; thus, Guard flying units once again no longer existed as a National Guard entity.

North American Aviation, Inc. BC-1, similar to the one flown by the 24th Observation Squadron. (*National Museum of the USAF*)

Chapter One

Guard Aviation Reborn

Within months of the United States entering World War II, the War Department started general deliberations of the Army's structure in postwar America.

The U.S. Constitution recognized the militia (National Guard) as a public institution in its militia clause. The National Defense Act of 1920 requires that the War Department include National Guard and Reserve officer input into the Department's planning, where that planning impacts both of these reserve components. In spite of these requirements, between 1941 and 1943, National Guard representation lost ground.

By mid-1943, the War Department started to set up committees to plan postwar requirements. Also, at the mid-year point, the Army Air Forces initiated their own planning. From this point through most of 1944, the Army Air Forces' goal was to become an independent branch of the military. The primacy of the bomber started to build prior to the war and, with their successes in Europe at this point in 1944, the Army Air Forces could only envision a large strategic bomber force being the thrust in the postwar Air Force. With this mind set, the National Guard and Reserves were not needed.

Army Chief of Staff General George C. Marshall foresaw a much smaller army than some of his army planners, and found the Army Air Forces' plan out of the question. Even a compromise plan of August 1944 between the Army and Army Air Forces displeased General Marshall, and he sent them back to the drawing board.

Though the Army Air Forces started to consider a Guard component in their plans in mid-1944, their expectations of Guard performance was quite low.

General George C. Marshall, chief of staff, War Department. (*Library of Congress*)

From the late 1944 "try again" order of General Marshall, it took about a year for all concerned to develop an acceptable plan. The resolution of the factions within the War Department came on August 27, 1945—the day that Third Fleet commander, Fleet Admiral William F. "Bull" Halsey, sailed into Tokyo's Sugami Bay with 23 aircraft carriers, 12 battleships, 26 cruisers, and over 300 smaller ships (V-J Day was on August 15, 1945).

The agreed upon policy proposals were approved by the Secretary of War October 13, 1945. Officially it was the "War Department Policies Relating to the

Post War National Guard and Organized Reserve Corps." The shorter title "Approved Policies 1945" was soon in use.

The aviation units of the National Guard were to share the Army Air Forces' Mobilization Day (M-Day) responsibilities. As an M-Day organization, they were to be capable of reaching wartime manning and equipment levels, as well as being operationally ready within a short time.

General Henry H. "Hap" Arnold, chief of the Army Air Forces. (*U.S. Army*)

All planning foresaw the Army Air Forces becoming an independent service and the National Guard to have two branches, air and army (ground). By mid-December 1945, the National Guard Bureau had formed an Aviation Group.

As the war was concluding, the state governors, in conjunction with their state adjutant generals, entered the fray to get Guard air units. Iowa's governor, Robert D. Blue, and Adjutant General, Brigadier General Charles H. Grahl, worked with the National Guard Bureau in Washington, D.C., to get such air units for Iowa. General Grahl had something to offer—the Sioux City Army Air Base, which had been closed the previous year. At the end of January 1946, General Grahl wrote Congressman Charles B. Hoeven of this possibility.

Iowa had some past success in lobbying for military aviation. In 1940, they successfully got a National Guard observation squadron (the 124th) for Des Moines. That same year they started their effort to cash in on the Army Air Forces' base expansion effort in the Midwest, which came to fruition the following year as the Sioux City Army Air Base in northwest Iowa.

On January 30, 1946, General of the Armies Dwight D. Eisenhower, Army Chief of Staff, ordered

132nd Fighter Group in the mid-1940s. (*132nd Fighter Wing*)

Republic P-47D Thunderbolt, the type of aircraft used by the 365th Fighter Group and its 386th Fighter Squadron during World War II. (*Air Force Historical Research Agency*)

the piecemeal activation of National Guard aviation units. A little more than a week later, the National Guard Bureau issued a memorandum to the Adjutant Generals of all states, the Territories of Hawaii and Puerto Rico, and the District of Columbia listing proposed numerical designations of aviation units, as well as proposed locations. Under the 57th Wing, Headquarters and Headquarters Squadron (St. Louis, Missouri) was the 132nd Fighter Group (Des Moines, Iowa), with the 124th Fighter Squadron, Single Engine (Des Moines, Iowa); 173rd Fighter Squadron, Single Engine (Omaha, Nebraska); 174th Fighter Squadron, Single Engine (Sioux City, Iowa); and 175th Fighter Squadron, Single Engine (Sioux Falls, South Dakota). The proposed unit designations were allocated to the National Guard May 24, 1946.

As it would turn out, Iowa's 132nd Fighter Group would end up consisting of the 124th, 173rd, and 174th Fighter Squadrons, SE. The 173rd Fighter Squadron, SE was the first to receive formal federal recognition of the 132nd Fighter Group. It was also the second of all National Guard air units to receive federal recognition; Colorado's 120th Fighter Squadron, SE was the first National Guard air unit to receive recognition on June 30, 1946.

These National Guard air units had lineage traced back to World War II units. The 124th Fighter Squadron, SE was the only one retaining its prewar designation, as it was originally one of the National Guard observation squadrons. The 132nd Fighter Group came from the 365th Fighter Group; Iowa's 174th Fighter Squadron, SE came from the 386th Fighter Squadron, part of the 365th Fighter Group; and Nebraska's 173rd Fighter Squadron, SE came from the 401st Fighter Squadron of the 370th Fighter Group.

To command the 132nd Fighter Group, Governor Robert D. Blue appointed Colonel Lester G. Orcutt, who was director of the Iowa Aeronautics Commission at the time and a past commander of Iowa National Guard's 124th Observation Squadron. Unfortunately, the War Department had an age limit on that position of 45 years, and Colonel Orcutt was 47. Nominated and accepted by the War Department for that position was Colonel Ellis E. Eno.

On August 23, 1946, both the 132nd Fighter Group and its 124th Fighter Squadron, SE, both based at Des Moines Municipal Airport, received federal recognition; the 174th Fighter Squadron, SE, stationed at part of the World War II Sioux City Army Air Base and adjoining to the Sioux City Municipal Airport, received their federal recognition December 2, 1946. The air base was a training base for B-17, B-24, and B-29 bomber crews.

Probably the most famous person to go through training at the Sioux City Army Air Base during World War II was actor turned pilot, and unit commander, Jimmy Stewart. (*USAF*)

Chapter 2

Sioux City Air Unit Organized

By late 1945, the War Department and the Army Air Forces finally agreed on a postwar plan which included the National Guard—with air units—and the Organized Reserve. The federal mission of the National Guard air units was an M-Day organization with an air defense orientation. The M-Day designation meant that they would be capable of rapid expansion to wartime manning and equipment levels, and to be fully operational ready. This would not be a reality for years.

Along with the War Department and Army Air Forces planners was the National Guard Bureau. Through the Bureau, the individual state and territorial governors and respective adjutant generals were kept appraised of the planning.

For the air units of the National Guard, the federal government would furnish aircraft, supplies, instructors, and pay. Most of the aircraft would be fighters (some light bombers). The Army Air Forces felt that the Guard was best suited for fighters because of their size, relatively low maintenance cost, and versatility. It was also thought by some that the excess of relatively capable fighters from the war played into the planning.

States would first have the right to accept or reject air units in National Guard Bureau recommendations. If the air unit was accepted, the states would furnish the manpower, base, and storage facilities. Selection of bases was accomplished by the state's adjutants general in coordination with state officials and local politicians. It was recommended that bases be near populated areas in order to enhance recruitment.

By early January 1946, based on state population, it was being presumed that Iowa would get two fighter squadrons. A number of cities in Iowa, including Burlington, Cedar Rapids, Davenport, Des Moines, and Sioux City, were vying for a National Guard air unit. Des Moines and Sioux City seemed to have advantages over the other cities. The only National Guard observation squadron in Iowa, the 124th, had a hangar at Des Moines Municipal Airport. Sioux City had a large World War II bomber crew training base.

Congressman Charles B. Hoeven wrote Iowa's adjutant general, Brigadier General Charles H. Grahl, in support of the use of the deactivated Sioux City Army Air Base in January. According to General Grahl's response to the congressman, as well as in a January 30, 1946, article in the *Sioux City Journal* newspaper, he stated that Sioux City and Des Moines were the primary candidates. He also indicated that one or both of Iowa's two squadrons might be split, with part of them going to one or two of the other cities desiring an air unit.

The same day that the above newspaper article came out, General of the Armies Dwight D. Eisenhower, Army Chief of Staff, gave the order to activate the National Guard air units. In early March, General Grahl announced that Brigadier General Gordon C. Hollar was to chair a committee to make plans to reorganize the postwar Iowa National Guard. Within the committee's planning were two air units, presumably one each at Sioux City and Des Moines.

By late March, General Grahl, Iowa Governor Robert D. Blue, and Sioux City Mayor Forrest M. Olson were discussing availability of portions of the air base to support 25 fighter aircraft along with 312 personnel. There were ample hangars, shops,

Today's view of the Air National Guard Base/Sioux Gateway Airport-Bud Day Field. (*185th ARW photo/McCallum collection*)

office space, and storage space available. Official state approval was still needed before recruiting could start.

In April, the National Guard Board requested use of the former Army Air Base in Sioux City. In the request was a requirement for 25 of the air base buildings. Among the buildings was hangar 802, which stood 140 feet by 110 feet. The other buildings included a smaller hangar, machine shop, link trainer building, warehouses, and a number of smaller facilities.

The old air base was connected to the Sioux City Municipal Airport. Walter E. Betsworth, airport manager, stated that the Guard and the city would share the expense of field operations, and that the part of the former air base the Guard was requesting had been reserved by the Army for Guard use when the base was turned over to the city in 1945.

Recruiting formally began in the first half of July. The Sioux City Junior Chamber of Commerce set up an information center for men interested in the air unit. The Sioux City air unit was to include the 174th Fighter Squadron, Single Engine, and an aircraft control and warning squadron. The 174th Fighter Squadron, SE was to have 25 P-51Hs (they would actually get P-51Ds), four A-26s, one C-47, two AT-6s, and two L-5s. Dean W. J. Scarborough, of Morningside College in Sioux City, was appointed

Mid-1940s view of Sioux City Army Air Base/Municipal Airport. (*U.S. Army Air Forces*)

by Gaylord Smith, president of the Junior Chamber of Commerce, to accept recruiting applications. Only applications of war veterans would be accepted.

October 1946 saw the beginning of the 174th Fighter Squadron, SE. On the 18th, Captain Roger Gilbert, recruiting officer in charge of the Guard's air office in the Sioux City armory, announced that the following units, along with the strength of each, would be formed in the Sioux City area:

174th Fighter Squadron, SE; 32 officers and 101 enlisted men

174th Utility Flight; 6 officers and 29 enlisted men

174th Weather Station, Type A; 3 officers and 5 enlisted men

Detachment B, 232nd Air Service Group; 9 officers and 168 enlisted men

232nd Air Service Group HQ and Detachment A were stationed at Des Moines (Detachment A supported the 124th Fighter Squadron, SE).

General Grahl announced on October 24th that Lieutenant Colonel Morgan R. Harrison, a World War II veteran then residing in Sioux City, was appointed commanding officer of the 174th Fighter Squadron, SE. Colonel Harrison held a recruiting meeting at the Sioux City National Guard armory on October 28th, at which 15 recruits were signed up. They took their physical examinations at the armory the following evening. The first recruit to sign up was Army Air Forces veteran Paul H. Tyler.

The recruits would start training as soon as the 174th was federally recognized. Federal recognition would take place when twenty-five percent of the authorized officers and ten percent of the enlisted men were present for duty. It took them just about a month to reach this goal, including the paperwork. Federal recognition was received on December 2, 1946, at the Sioux City armory. At this time they had 16 officers, 9 rated (pilots), and 46 enlisted men.

For the month of January 1947, Colonel Harrison and the 174th Fighter Squadron operated out of the armory. Here recruiting, organizing the squadron, and making assignments, as well as training, took up their time. Planning for their anticipated move to the air base was of high priority. Equipment and supplies were requested. Coordination with the 132nd Fighter Group in Des Moines was a constant item.

Lt. Col. Morgan R. Harrison was commander of the 174th Fighter Squadron, SE between December 2, 1946, to September 1, 1947. (*174th FS/McCallum collection*)

The big day arrived. On February 1st, the squadron took up residence at the air base in the large World War II hangar. They were not the first unit to arrive at the air base. The 140th Reserve Training Detachment, part of the Organized Reserve, was activated at the base the previous July 31st. Soon after their arrival at the air base, they received their first two aircraft, North American AT-6 trainers. On February 12th, the first eight of 25 North American P-51D Mustang fighters to be assigned to them arrived.

The hangar housing the Guard flyers was not totally usable. In 1945, while the base was part of the war effort, a fire damaged the hangar. Funds would be obtained ($70,000) through the National Guard Bureau for repairs. It would be over a year for the repair effort to be completed.

The squadron was still in need of additional personnel. They would not reach the halfway point until the following year. With the personnel at hand

The World War II air base hangar was part of the base given to the 174th FS to operate from. (*Stolze photo/McCallum collection*)

The first aircraft received by the 174th FS in early 1947 were L-5s and T-6s. (*Stolze photo/McCallum collection*)

The large air base hangar had been damaged by an aircraft fire before the Army Air Forces moved out. Here the huge telephone polls that were holding it up can be clearly seen. P-51D 079 was one of the first fighters to arrive for the 174th. (*Stolze photo/ McCallum collection*)

— mostly World War II veterans — they found time between training and installing the unit at the air base to put on two air shows jointly with the 140th Reserve Training Detachment. The first was in April, in celebration of Army Week, and the second was in August, to celebrate the Army Air Forces' 40th anniversary, along with the 140th's one year anniversary.

A change of command came September 1, 1947, when Lieutenant Colonel Harrison was replaced by Major J. Allen Orr. Harrison was transferring into the regulars. Orr, like Harrison, was in World War II, flying bombers in the Pacific.

Major J. Allen Orr commanded the 174th FS between September 1, 1947, and August 1, 1948. (*174th FS/McCallum collection*)

September was also a milestone in American aviation. On the 18th, the United States Air Force became a separate military service and the Air National Guard became a reserve component of the Air Force. This was brought about by the National Security Act of 1947, which became law June 26th of that year.

The 174th Fighter Squadron celebrated its first anniversary December 2, 1947. At that time, they had a total of 36 aircraft, 28 officers, and168 enlisted men, which included 35 caretakers—full time personnel who later would be called air technicians. The squadron's full manning was 45 officers and 303 enlisted men for years.

Aircraft of the 174th Fighter Squadron

Flight line on a snowy winter's day. Not unusual for the Midwest. (*Stolze photo/McCallum collection*)

Assignment of aircraft for the first years was for the P-51 to be assigned to the squadron and the support aircraft assigned to the Utility Flight. The Utility Flight aircraft included A-26s, as shown here, as well as the L-5s, T-6s, and C-47. (*Stolze photo/McCallum collection*)

Outside winter maintenance on the C-47. (*Stolze photo/McCallum collection*)

By the time the 174th received their T-6 and P-51 aircraft, the national insignia had been changed to incorporate a red stripe in the bars. The Guard took some time incorporating this change. (*Stolze photo/McCallum collection*)

Operating Around Reconstrucation

Repair work on the interior of the large hangar and expansion on the outside took a good bit of time during 1947/1948. (*Stolze photo/ McCallum collection*)

Flight operations beside the construction area. (*Stolze photo/ McCallum collection*)

The Mission

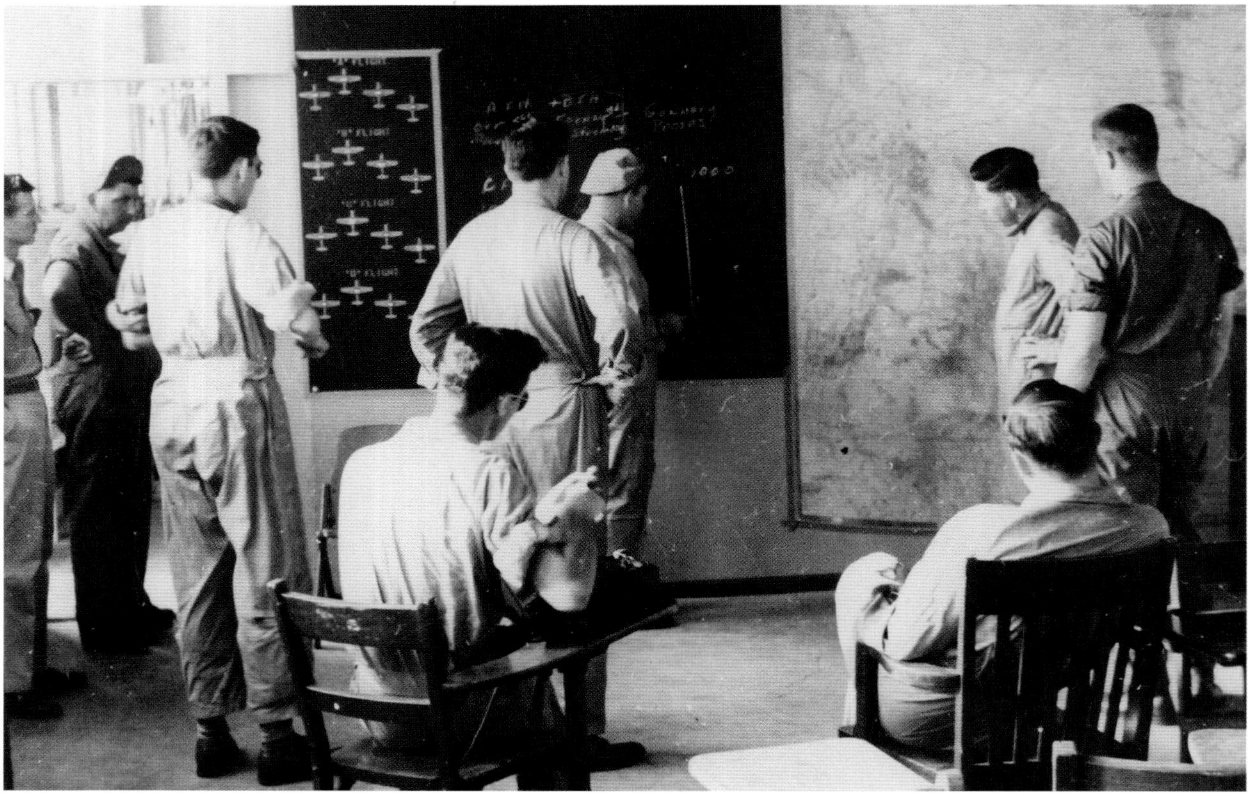

The briefing. (*Stolze photo/McCallum collection*)

A Cletrac moves a P-51D into position for a flight. (*Stolze photo/McCallum collection*)

Pilots John S. Bradley and Gale D. V. Stevens take off on the day's mission. (*Stolze photo/McCallum collection*)

Mission completed. (*Stolze photo/McCallum collection*)

Chapter 3

Entering the Jet Age

As 1948 opened, the 174th Fighter Squadron, SE had only recruited 62 percent of the officers and 55 percent of the enlisted men needed for full staffing. This was a common problem in most Guard units. There were plenty of experienced World War II veterans, but limits on Air National Guard ranks proved to be a problem. Because of the slow staffing, combined with funding and equipment shortages, the U.S. Air Force did not deem any Air Guard units as operationally ready. Such terms as "flying clubs" and "aircraft in flyable storage" were being bandied about.

Early squadron sign hung up in the coffee shop. (*Stolze photo/ McCallum collection*)

In good Midwest "can do" fashion, the 174th Fighter Squadron pressed on. In August, they held their first two-week annual field training. This first one was held on-base in Sioux City, while the pilots flew their F-51 Mustangs to Rapid City, South Dakota, for gunnery practice.

It should be noted that in June 1948, the U.S. Air Force modified their aircraft designation system. This affected the 174th Fighter Squadron, in that the P-51 became the F-51, the A-26 became the B-26 (not to be confused with the Martin B-26 of World War II), and the AT-6 became the T-6.

Major Orr was promoted to operations officer of the 132nd Fighter Group in Des Moines. Replacing him was Major Robert E. Ruby, who had been operations officer of the 124th Fighter Squadron, SE in Des Moines. Although the change in command was effective August 1, 1948, it was not announced until August 14th.

The winter of 1948/1949 was quite brutal from the Rockies east through Nebraska. That September and October, the weather was quite nice and the farmers were able to get all their crops in. The weather changed drastically November 18th, and by early January, the "Blizzard of 1949" hit. Over a wide area thousands of cattle and sheep were stranded and starving. U.S. Air Force, Air Force Reserve, and Air National Guard planes and personnel participated in Operation Haylift, air dropping bundles of hay to these animals. The 174th Utility Flight C-47 and crew aided in this humanitarian effort.

As 1949 reached its midpoint, the 174th Fighter Squadron started making plans for their August two-

Fueling the 174th's aircraft under winter conditions could be a challenge. (*Stolze photo/McCallum collection*)

Major Robert C. Ruby was squadron commander between August 14, 1948, and January 1952. Possibly one of the interesting scrambles at this time was in search of flying saucers. (*174th FS*)

The NG, for National Guard, has been added to this aircraft's markings. (*Stolze photo/McCallum collection*)

Snow removal was required to allow winter operations. (*Stolze photo/McCallum collection*)

week field training. At about this time, word came that they would transition into jet fighters. It was thought that they would receive Republic F-84B Thunderjets by the end of the year.

To prepare for their new aircraft, three officers were selected for Air Force transition training: Major Robert C. Ruby, the squadron's commanding officer; Captain John S. Bradley, operations officer; and Lieutenant Harry L. McGraw. Prior to transition training they had to go through pressure chamber tests. As Sioux City Air Base did not have such facilities, they went to Vance AFB, Enid, Oklahoma (name changed from Enid AFB to Vance AFB July 9, 1949).

In October, the three officers went to Williams AFB, Chandler, Arizona, where they were part of a class of 50 Air National Guard pilots from a number of states. This three-week course consisted of a few classroom sessions, time in a Captivair trainer, dual time in a Lockheed T-33 trainer, and finally, solo flight time in the single-seat Lockheed F-80 Shooting Star fighter.

The Captivair trainer was an F-80 securely attached to the ground by steel-enforced concrete

In preparation for F-84B operations, some of the pilots were sent to Phoenix, Arizona, for jet conversion training. (*174th FS*)

supports. The aircraft's instrumentation were linked to instruments in a control house, where instructor personnel could monitor and evaluate the pilot in simulated flight.

During the remaining months of 1949, Captains Don W. Forney and Malcolm L. McMillan went through the same training. These five Air National Guard officers, along with Lieutenant Colonel Charles G. Teschner, U.S. Air Force senior air instructor, would be instructors and provide ground training for the rest of the squadron pilots.

The F-84Bs and F-84Cs scheduled for Air Guard squadrons had to go through a multi-million dollar modification and modernization program at the Republic plant. This took longer than initially planned. This slow-up in aircraft rework, plus shortages in ground support equipment, meant delays in delivery, including the 174th. They would not see theirs in 1949.

Besides their federal military mission, Air Guard has state responsibilities which include assisting in time of disasters. There was a thriving cattle business in the Sioux City Stock Yards. This included a number of processing plants and offices in the Yards area. One of these concerns was Swift and Company, which had offices and some processing work done in a six-story building on Leech Avenue. On December 14, 1949, at 11:33 a.m., a great explosion caused major damage to this building.

The explosion wreaked havoc on the building. Twenty-one people died, with nearly 100 injured. The National Guard was mobilized at the governor's order. About 100 of the 174th Fighter Squadron members volunteered in the disaster relief effort. The Air Guard's huge airplane wrecker was used in clearing heavy steel girders away so rescuers could get to the injured and dead.

In anticipation of receiving the Republic F-84B, the 174th Fighter squadron started their in-house ground school for the squadron pilots in January 1950. The squadron pilots that had completed the U.S. Air Force transition course the year before, along with the U.S. Air Force air instructor, acted as instructors in the ground training. Here the squadron pilots learned basic jet operations and specifics on the F-84B.

174th's Major John S. Bradley and one of the F-80s used in the jet training program. (*174th FS*)

For nearly a year, the squadron had been expecting jets. There had been a number of false alarms, in which rumors of imminent arrival of the F-84 failed to materialize and brought about much disappointment. Then, on the afternoon of April 8, 1950, the wooshing of jets came to the ears of those on base, and most of Sioux City. Much to everyone's delight, Air Force pilots landed the two jets. The question on many an airmen's lips was, were they theirs? Yes!

The next few weeks were quite busy. By the 30th, the squadron had 16 of the F-84Bs, with another 10 expected by the end of May. About 13 of the squadron pilots had completed the in-house ground school and 16 had been jet qualified. With their new aircraft, the squadron was redesignated the 174th Fighter Squadron, Jet May 1st.

War clouds soon overcame the nation. On June 25, 1950, the North Koreans invaded their neighbor to the south. Soon after a debate started within the U.S. Air Force as to whether to call up the Air Guard or not and, if so, how. It was decided in early September to mobilize the Air Guard, and in less than a week the 123rd Fighter Group of the Kentucky Air National Guard was notified.

In 1946, the Air Guard was organized as an M-Day air defense force that would need very little post-mobilization training. The war, under this scenario, was a prolonged World War II type. In 1949, the Continental Air Command, which oversaw the Air National Guard, Reserves, and Continental U.S.

Lineup of squadron aircraft. The national insignia has been updated, and "Iowa" and "NG" have been added to the fuselage. (*Stolze photo/McCallum collection*)

One of the F-84Bs assigned to the 174th. Note the change from NG to ANG has been applied. (*Stolze photo/McCallum collection*)

1949 summer camp at Volk Field, Wisconsin. (*Stolze photo/ McCallum collection*)

air defense responsibilities, found during inspection of Air Guard fighter units that the Air Guard would take nearly three months of post-mobilization training to make them operationally ready.

The mobilization of Air Guard units, which started in October, brought about another problem; the structure of Air Guard units differed from the "combat wing" structure used by the regular Air Force and proved difficult in attempting to integrate the Guard and the USAF. Because in the Air Guard the various units in each state could be quite a distance apart, a modified combat wing structure was agreed upon. One problem seemed to lead to another. With the new structure agreed upon, increases in manning would be needed. But most Air Guard units were already understaffed, due to lack of budgets and other requirements that seemed to hinder recruitment.

For Iowa, the 132nd Wing Headquarters and Headquarters Squadron was constituted and allotted to the National Guard Bureau September 1, 1950. On November 1st, the 132nd Wing was federally recognized. The 132nd Wing consisted of the 132nd Medical Group, 132nd Air Base Group, 132nd Maintenance and Supply Group, and the 132nd

F-84B 46-599 has been pulled into the Guard's hangar for inspection and training. (*Stolze photo/McCallum collection*)

The maintenance personnel are an integral element in squadron operations. Here the 50 cal. guns on the F-51 are being boresighted. (*Stolze photo/McCallum collection*)

Rockets are loaded in anticipation of air-to-ground gunnery during summer camp. (*Stolze photo/McCallum collection*)

Another F-84B has arrived, and both pilot and crew chief give it the once-over. (*Stolze photo/McCallum collection*)

Fit check. There was some concern within the squadron as to the possibility of a pilot losing his feet and/or legs upon ejection in an emergency. Here pilot Paul Cook, who reportedly had the largest feet, is helping to check the operation out. Observing the operation is squadron commander Major Ruby. (*Stolze photo/McCallum collection*)

A whole flock of F-51s has taken roost in the 174th's large hangar. Note the absence of the national insignia on the aircraft. (*Stolze photo/McCallum collection*)

Fighter Group. Gone were the 232nd Air Service Group and its detachments. On that same November 1st, the 174th Fighter Squadron, Jet was authorized to increase manning to meet increased responsibility of support. The Utility Flight was disbanded that October 31dy, and its aircraft and personnel were integrated into the fighter squadron. As a recruiting effort, the 174th Fighter Squadron, Jet held an open house called "The 174th Jet Fighters On Review" October 22nd.

The final month of 1950, along with early January 1951, the squadron had two thoughts: becoming proficient in their new jets, and when or if they would be mobilized. On January 19, 1951, the call came from the 132nd Fighter Wing headquarters that they were given ten weeks' notice of their formal call to active duty. This included Wing Headquarters, 124th Fighter Squadron, SE (Des Moines); 173rd Fighter Squadron, Jet (Lincoln, Nebraska); and the 174th Fighter Squadron, Jet (Sioux City).

In the midst of preparation for mobilization, disaster struck Sioux City Municipal Airport March 2, 1951. Mid-Continent Airlines Flight 16, a DC-3A, had originated in Kansas City, Missouri, at 7:24 a.m. Its final destination was Minneapolis, Minnesota, with a number of intermediate stops, including Sioux City, Iowa. As the plane approached Sioux City Municipal Airport, the weather was bad—a snow storm with winds, low ceiling, and one mile visibility. The pilot missed the runway on his first attempt. He attempted a turn around to try again. It is believed that a stall occurred as he was making

Star of the October 22, 1949, open house is the F-84B. (*Stolze photo/McCallum collection*)

Disassembled for training, these F-84s drew quite a crowd. F-51 operations continued as training went on with the F-84. (*Stolze photo/McCallum collection*)

his turn, and due to close proximity to the ground he could not recover.

The DC-3A crashed about 600 feet northwest of the approach end of Runway 17. Air Guard personnel on the same airfield as the Municipal Airport found the crash site difficult to locate in the snow storm. Besides the Air Guard and other airport personnel, all of Sioux City's fire equipment and 11 ambulances made it to the scene. Of the 25 occupants on the plane, nine survived.

April 1, 1951, Headquarters 132nd Fighter Wing, Special Orders Number 8, paragraph 15.1: "The 174th Fighter Squadron, Jet, having been ordered into the active military service...."

Happenings at the base

An F-51 is pulled out from the large hangar by a Cletrac. (*Stolze photo/McCallum collection*)

There was enough room for both F-51 and F-84 aircraft in the hangar. When the weather was bad enough they could maneuver all of their aircraft into the hangar. (*Stolze photo/McCallum collection*)

Engine maintenance was much easier in the hangar. Cold winters and hot summers added a difficulty factor when working in the outdoors. Maybe not climate controlled, but the hangar gave shelter from the elements. (*Stolze photo/McCallum collection*)

Engine maintenance meant removing the aft fuselage/tail section from the F-84B. (*Stolze photo/McCallum collection*)

Going operational with the F-84B. (*Stolze photo/McCallum collection*)

Still carrying USAF markings, ANG markings would eventually replace them. (*Stolze photo/McCallum collection*)

Chapter 4

Active Duty

Post-World War II planning anticipated another prolonged, all-out war like the last. When the North Koreans invaded South Korea on June 25, 1950, the U.S. Air Force had not yet completed its mobilization planning and had not anticipated a war such as this. Initially, the Air Force and others thought this conflict, or police action, would soon be over.

Because of the expected short duration of the Korean conflict, there was not a call-up of all Air National Guard units. What units were ordered into federal service were viewed by the Air Force as a temporary measure, or stop-gap action, until the regulars could come up to strength, and then the Guard could be sent home. But they had miscalculated. In November, a large force of communist Chinese crossed the Yalu River and entered the fray. It was back to the drawing board. Was the Korean action a diversion for some Soviet action in Europe?

For a while, it looked as if the allied forces might be pushed off the Korean peninsula. On December 16th, President Harry S. Truman declared a national emergency. Force strength in the regular and reserve services were authorized to be increased. Many more Air National Guard units would get call-up notification in January, February, and beyond.

Besides the Air Guard units activated in January, a number were given notice of impending call-up. On January 19, 1951, the 132nd Fighter Wing was given 10 weeks' notice; they would be activated April 1st. The call-up included the 132nd Fighter Wing headquarters stationed in Des Moines, Iowa; the 124th Fighter Squadron, SE, equipped with F-51Ds and stationed in Des Moines, Iowa; the 173rd Fighter Squadron, Jet, equipped with F-80Cs and stationed in Lincoln, Nebraska; and the 174th Fighter Squadron, Jet, equipped with F-84Bs and stationed in Sioux City, Iowa. The Air Force found that they lacked resources in many areas, including aircraft. They would take F-51s, F-80s, and F-84s from Air National Guard squadrons and reassign them either to Air Force or other Air Guard squadrons to meet immediate needs. The 173rd Fighter Squadron would lose their F-80Cs and be re-equipped with F-51Ds again. Prior to transferring to their active duty base, they were redesignated 173rd Fighter Squadron, SE on December 18, 1950. In October, the 174th Fighter Squadron saw the beginning of the transfer of a little more than 40 percent of their fighters prior to activation. In October, one F-84B went to the 128th Fighter Squadron, Georgia Air National Guard at Dobbins AFB. Between December 1950 and March 1951, nine of their F-84Bs went to the 197th Fighter Squadron, Arizona Air National Guard, Luke AFB.

The Air Guard units being called up were assigned to the various Air Force commands within the continental U.S. and overseas. Along with the 132nd Fighter Wing and its squadrons, New Jersey's 108th, Missouri's 131st, and California's 146th, along with two light bombardment wings (New York's 106th and Pennsylvania's 111th) were assigned to Strategic Air Command.

The ten weeks prior to activation was a busy time for the personnel of the 174th Fighter Squadron. Personally, those who were not employed full time at the Guard had to make arrangements at their civilian employment. There were many preparations at the family level, also. They were going to be on active duty and away from home for 21 months. On March 22nd, they were informed that they would be going to Dow AFB, Bangor, Maine, and that they would be under the Strategic Air Command. At the Sioux City base, there were the usual mounds of paperwork, along with the physical effort of preparing for activation. At the end of March, the 132nd Fighter Wing personnel, along with squadron representatives, flew to Dow AFB for meetings and inspection of the facilities.

April 1st came, and the 174th Fighter Squadron, with its officers and enlisted ranks, was no longer a state unit, but part of the U.S. Air Force. Those with civilian jobs were not full-time Air Guard. Until the actual move to Maine, they would continue to live in their homes.

A detachment was sent to Strategic Air Command headquarters at Offutt AFB, Omaha, Nebraska, to preprocess some personnel prior to the April 1st call-up. After April 1st, the majority of squadron personnel would be processed in Sioux City.

As it would turn out, they would have about 15 days before departure to Dow AFB. During this time, physicals were given and personnel processing was accomplished. During this two week period, the

Eighteen of the squadron's 27 pilots appear in this March 1951 photo. First row: 1st Lt. Sheldon W. Hanneman, 1st Lt. Warren G. Nelson, 2nd Lt. Harold L. Taylor, Jr., and Maj. John S. Bradley; Second row: Capt. Richard M. Baughn, Capt. Harry L. Mc Graw, 1st Lt. Thomas E. Green, 1st Lt. Jack A. Savage, 1st Lt. Richard P. Sulzbach, and 1st Lt. Alfred C. Grier. Third row: Capt. Donald W. Forney, 1st Lt. Richard J. Smith, 1st Lt. Kelly F. Cook, Maj. Malcolm L. McMillan, Capt. Don A. Oldis, Major Robert C. Ruby (CO), 1st Lt. Douglas C. Griggs, and 1st Lt. Richard C. Nurre. (*174th FS/McCallum collection*)

174th Fighter Squadron mechanics in March 1951. (*174th FS/McCallum collection*)

squadron pilots flew their remaining 14 F-84Bs to Dow AFB. At Sioux City there was a lot of packing, crating, and loading of supplies and equipment on trucks and trains. The bulky items were shipped by rail, while some of the lighter items went by truck. The squadron and its equipment left Sioux City April 12th (some elements left as early as April 5th).

Dow AFB had been a World War II base where bombers staged out for flights overseas. It was deactivated in November 1949, but the Korean War brought the need to reactivate it again. This occurred February 1, 1951.

When most of the 132nd Fighter Wing arrived at Dow AFB on April 25th, they found the base was in sad shape. The installation as a whole needed major repair. A lot of time and money had to be spent to get it functionally ready, including contracting for repairs to make it livable.

The 174th Fighter Squadron, as well as all the 132nd Fighter Wing, expected to receive training in their new bomber escort mission. Both the 124th and 173rd squadrons anticipated turning in their F-51s for more modern jets.

Though they had a mission as bomber-escort, none of the four Air Guard wings under Strategic Air Command were so designated. The 108th and 131st Fighter Wings, activated on March 1st, were redesignated Fighter-Bomber Wings in April, while the 132nd and 146th Fighter Wings, activated on April 1st, were redesignated Fighter-Bomber Wings on June 1st. Not only did the 132nd Fighter Wing's 124th and 173rd Fighter Squadrons' hope of getting jets evaporate, but the 174th Fighter Squadron would soon find that they, too, would be losing their jet fighters. They would find that their aircraft would be going to Maine's 132nd Fighter Squadron. Ten were assigned to the 132nd Fighter Squadron that April, three more by June 1st, and the last in November. With the loss of their jets they, too, were re-equipped with F-51Ds. Morale in the 132nd Fighter Wing was hitting a very low point.

While under Strategic Air Command, the 132nd Fighter (later Fighter-Bomber) Wing flew training missions. On May 8, 1951, while flying on one of these missions, 174th Fighter Squadron pilot 1st Lieutenant Thomas E. Green, a World War II veteran, got caught up in nasty weather, lost his radios as well as his location, and soon found himself low on fuel. He had two choices: bail out or find a place to land. Landing was not an easy choice. The area was quite wooded, and there were not many suitable locations. Lieutenant Green chose to land. Fortunately, he found a suitable area, circled it, and brought his F-84B down with no injury to himself, other than frayed nerves, and not much damage to his aircraft. In October, the Wing participated in a long range mission with their F-51Ds. They remained airborne in excess of seven hours. This was a night flight between Bangor, Maine, and Raleigh, North Carolina, then back to Bangor. They flew a total distance of over 1,600 miles.

174th Fighter Squadron flight line, Dow AFB, Bangor, Maine. None of the F-84Bs are shown, just the replacement F-51. (*Stolze photo/McCallum collection*)

The Wing's pilots were not the only ones to receive training. A great number of the enlisted men were young—high school and college age—with no military training. About 150 of them received basic training at Dow AFB in June.

Strategic Air Command felt that the four ex-Air National Guard fighter wings were having difficulty transitioning to the SAC mission, and that their experience and training would be more amenable to the ground support mission. All four wings were notified in mid-November that they were being transferred to Tactical Air Command.

The 132nd Fighter-Bomber Wing transferred to Tactical Air Command Wednesday, November 16th. That following Monday, Colonel John H. Holmes, Wing commander, and several of his key staff went to Pope AFB in North Carolina for a two-day meeting. At the meeting, Colonel Holmes and his staff found out that the Wing would be moving to Alexandria AFB, initially scheduled for February 1952.

Now under Tactical Air Command, they would be flying a different set of missions. The first came around the time of the change of command announcement; the 174th, along with the rest of the Wing, flew their F-51Ds to Montagorta Island, in the Gulf of Mexico off of Texas, for aerial gunnery. Not much is in the historical records of this mission, save the remembrances of one of the sergeants at Montagorta as part of the squadron's support personnel. He remembered the "mosquitos, soured ducks, smoke bombs, fire extinguishers, and horseplay."

The 174th had low morale when they lost their Thunderjets, but more was to come. Between December 24th and the 27th, Air Guard pilots assigned at call-up were transferred out. Sixteen of the jet pilots and a supply officer went to NATO forces in Europe: most to the 20th Fighter Wing stationed at Langley AFB, Virginia. These latter pilots would spend most of their time with the 20th Fighter Wing in Europe. Eight more pilots went to Korea, while two non-rated officers went to Far East Air Command.

These pilots' slots would be filled with returning Korean veterans. Major Ruby, the squadron's commander, chose to stay in the active Air Force in January. He would become the commanding officer of the 36th Fighter-Bomber Squadron in May 1952, flying missions out of Suwon AB (K13) in Korea. A number of the Air Guard pilots would choose to remain in the active Air Force. On January 7, 1952, Major Rollin M. Batten, who had been with Nebraska's 173rd Fighter-Bomber Squadron, became commander of the 174th.

The new year started with a bang for the 174th's new commanding officer and the mostly replacement pilots now manning its aircraft. Since about the time that the 132nd Fighter-Bomber Wing was transferred to Tactical Air Command, the Command and the Army had started the planning phase of a joint winter exercise called SNOW FALL. In SNOW FALL, the scenario is that an aggressor invades the eastern U.S. under winter conditions. The

Major Rollin M. Batten, Jr. was transferred from the 173rd Fighter Squadron to the 174th in February 1952 to take over command of the latter. (*Stolze photo/McCallum collection*)

By the time Operation Snowfall came about, only the maintenance personnel of the original 174th Fighter Squadron were at Dow AFB. The pilots flying the replacement F-51Ds (in place of the F-84Bs) were "rep:acements" themselves. The 174th pilots that had been mobilized in Iowa had been sent to other units, mostly the 20th Fighter Wing. (*Stolze photo/McCallum collection*)

Washing down the engine. At this time, the practice of using gasoline to wash aircraft and the engine was quite common. This practice is no longer in use. (*Stolze photo/McCallum collection*)

purpose is to train Air Force and Army units under such conditions in individual survival; planning and executing offensive and defensive operations; airborne operations; tactical air operations, air, motor, and rail movement; and logistics support.

This cold-weather exercise was held at Camp Drum, New York. Army, Air Force (Tactical Air Command), and Reserve forces participated. Air Force forces and Tactical Air Division (Prov) were stationed at Wheeler-Sack Army Air Field at Camp Drum. The fighter-bomber and reconnaissance aircraft, along with the Aggressor aircraft, were based at Griffiss AFB, Rome, New York. The role of the 132nd Fighter-Bomber Wing is to supply 38 F-51s for the defenders and 12 for the aggressor force—both pilots and support personnel. The 124th and 173rd Fighter-Bomber Squadrons were the defenders, and 174th Fighter-Bomber Squadron flew the aggressor F-51s.To identify the Aggressor F-51s, the wing tips and upper portion of the tails were painted with red water paint.

During January and the first week of February, units slated for the exercise engaged in pre-exercise training. The Tactical Air Division (Provisional), including the F-51s, aimed at preparing the units for operations in areas of extreme cold, including indoctrination for survival in winter operations, the care and use of equipment under winter conditions, cold weather and over-snow operations, employment of and defense against atomic weapons, and Joint Army-Air Force tactics. They would fly orientation flights in the maneuver area, ground-controlled intercepts, and cover and escort missions of troop carrier aircraft, as well as individual proficiency flights.

The exercise itself took place between February 8th and the 15th. The F-51s flew 65 air superiority missions, 57 interdiction missions, and 114 close

Crew chief Lee-on-ski Lar-son-a-vitch seems appropriate for war games where you are playing the part of a Russian aggressor. (*Stolze photo/McCallum collection*)

air support missions, as well as flying cover for the troop carrier aircraft with 11th Airborne Division drops. The report on Aggressor Close Support Operations stated:

> Aggressor close support operations were carried out by 12 F-51s drawn from the 132nd Fighter-Bomber Wing. These operations were characterized by a considerable lack of realism. In the first place, the Aggressor fighter-bombers were drawn from the U.S. forces' fighter-bomber unit, the 132nd Wing. In the second place, because Aggressor and U.S. aircraft operated from the same base—Griffiss AFB—each could observe all activities of the other. From the standpoint of Aggressor air, the use of Griffiss was unrealistic, also in that it was located in enemy (U.S.) territory, many miles behind the U.S. Forces' front lines. A degree of realism was achieved by requiring Aggressor aircraft to make their penetrations of the U.S. zone from the east or northeast in order to create the illusion that the aircraft were coming from the Aggressor rear areas. There were occasions when the weather was bad at Griffiss but good in the rear of Aggressor front lines, yet Aggressor aircraft could not fly because Griffiss was weathered in.

The cold weather exercise did point out a number of problems for the F-51 personnel. The winter weather clothing issued to the ground crews were found to be inadequate for the time they had to spend in the adverse weather working on the

Another 174th turned Russian—Wilkinovski. (*Stolze photo/ McCallum collection*)

aircraft. The crews experienced difficulty in moving the C-21 and C-22 auxiliary power units across snow- or ice-covered surfaces. Tugs were needed to move them. Starting the units also proved to be a problem. Usually they could get one to start, and then by attaching a V-belt between the operating unit and one that was giving them problems, they could get the next to start. Problems with the aircraft themselves included ice and snow freezing on the sides of the fuselage, wing, and stabilizer; propellers developed oil leaks during the oil dilution periods; and wood chocks froze to the ramp.

The 174th Fighter-Bomber Squadron was back to Dow AFB barely a month when they were off again, this time to Eglin AFB, Florida. The 174th flew gunnery missions from one of Eglin's auxiliary fields. While at Eglin, the 174th participated in one of Tactical Air Command's bi-annual Fire Power Demonstrations. One of the highlights on this occasion was when one of the F-51s shot itself in the

Welcome to Louisiana. (*Stolze photo/McCallum collection*)

The new home for the 174th Fighter Squadron enlisted personnel, the barracks at Alexandria AFB. (*Stolze photo/McCallum collection*)

tail during an air-to-ground gunnery demonstration. Apparently, the pilot held on the target too long. As he pulled up, one of his last shots ricocheted up and hit him in the horizontal stabilizer.

By the end of April, the 132nd Wing had moving orders. Their next base would be Alexandria AFB, Louisiana (later to be named England AFB). On June 1st, an advanced detachment was at Alexandria, setting up operations and making preparations to receive the rest of the Wing. The F-51s which had been at Eglin AFB in Florida on gunnery practice had been flown to Alexandria earlier, and awaited the arrival of the rest of the Wing. The Personnel left Dow AFB by many modes of transportation: bus, rail, plane, car, house trailer, and motorcycle. The main body arrived June 11th, and they had to set up operations once again.

Their stay at Alexandria would turn out to be a short six months. While there, the 132nd Wing received second place honors in a 9th Air Force gunnery meet during one of their trips to Eglin AFB. The Air Force announced plans to release those airmen whose separation date was prior to January 1953. Indeed, releases started in November. On December 31st, the 132nd Fighter-Bomber Wing, along with Sioux City's 174th Fighter-Bomber Squadron, was returned to state control. The F-51s and most of the pilots (who were not of Sioux City, or necessarily the Air National Guard) and equipment stayed at Alexandria AFB, where the 366th Fighter-Bomber Group was formed January 1, 1953.

20th Fighter-Bomber Wing and the 174th Fighter-Bomber Squadron Pilots

There is a sub-story to the 174th's Korean call-up. Though the squadron remained within the U.S., a majority of the squadron pilots (20 of 27) were

The 174th flight line at one of the auxiliary fields for Eglin AFB, Florida. When the 174th is returned to state control, all of their aircraft will stay in Florida. (*Stolze photo/McCallum collection*)

Gear swing. (*Stolze photo/McCallum collection*)

Heat, humidity, and bugs could not stop the 174th from carrying out their mission. An engine change probably meant a good bit of weight loss from sweat. (*Stolze photo/McCallum collection*)

Propeller change. (*Stolze photo/McCallum collection*)

Maintenance tent city is in full operation. A number of F-51s are in the process of being readied for the day's missions. (*Stolze photo/ McCallum collection*)

Getting ready to do some flying over a bombing range. (*Stolze photo/McCallum collection*)

Loading the 50s. (*Stolze photo/McCallum collection*)

F-51 receiving its armament load for the day's mission over the range. (*Stolze photo/McCallum collection*)

transferred to the 20th Fighter-Bomber Wing, stationed at Langley AFB, Virginia. With the 20th, the Air Guard pilots from Iowa would gain the unique distinction of flying with the first nuclear-capable tactical fighter wing in the USAF.

From the start of the Korean war in June 1950, there was a wide-spread fear that the Soviet Union would use it as a diversion to distract the U.S. as they instigated military action in Europe. To bolster the North Atlantic Treaty Organization (NATO), the USAF sent the 20th Fighter-Bomber Group and its F-84Ds from its base at Shaw AFB, South Carolina, to Manston, England, in July 1950. They returned to the U.S. in December of that same year.

When the Soviets exploded their first nuclear bomb in 1949, the U.S. realized that they had to revise their European strategies. Strategic bombers were not the answer, tactical nuclear weapons were. This "forward strategy" for NATO, as it was known, was to counter possible Soviet aggression in that area. A lighter-weight bomb was needed for tactical aircraft, much lighter than the 10,000-pound bomb then carried by the big bombers. U.S. nuclear scientists came through with the 1,680-pound Mark 7 nuclear bomb, often referred to as the 30-inch nuclear bomb. This tactical nuclear bomb would be carried by a number or Air Force and Navy fighter and attack aircraft.

The swept-wing F-84F Thunderstreak was to be the next Republic tactical fighter in the F-84 family—a much-needed improvement. Unfortunately, when the Korean War broke out, the

Twentieth Fighter-Bomber Wing F-84Gs at Langley AFB preparing for their new nuclear mission. Most of the 174th Fighter Squadron pilots would be dispersed among the 20th's squadrons. (*National Museum of the USAF*)

A 20th Fighter-Bomber Wing F-84G receives fuel from a KB-29. (*National Museum of the USAF*)

F-model was suffering from design troubles. As a stopgap measure, what was basically an upgraded and improved F-84E was put together. This updated straight-wing F-84 incorporated the more powerful J35-A-29 engine, which produced 5,600 pounds of thrust; it had an automatic pilot, and was equipped with a receptacle in the left wing for aerial refueling via flying boom tankers.

The 20th Fighter-Bomber Wing moved from Shaw AFB to Langley AFB, Virginia, with their F-84D on November 19, 1951. The move was not much of a surprise. Earlier, the Wing's commanding officer, Colonel John A. Dunning, had told some of his staff that they would be making this move, and that they would be the first tactical unit with nuclear bombs. Meeting the Wing was seven of their members that had come to Langley earlier. This advance team had gone to Langley to learn about nuclear weapons and methods of delivery. Now their task was to pass that learning on to the rest of the Wing's pilots.

Things were moving fast. Soon after arriving, and still in November, they began to get the F-84Gs, augmenting their D models at first. They would get many more—around 100 of the craft. In December, the 20 pilots from the 174th Fighter-Bomber

The F-84G flown by the 20th Fighter-Bomber Wing was the first fighter capable of in-flight refueling and as a nuclear strike aircraft. In this instance the F-84 is being refueled by a KC-97. (USAF/20th Fighter Wing)

The Mark 7 was as lightweight as nuclear bombs went at the time; it weighed 1,680 pounds, and had a yield of about one kiloton. Its yield was small enough, in that it would not hamper friendly operations, but enough to give any aggressor food for thought. (USAF/20th Fighter Wing)

Here are some of the returning 174th, late of the 20th F-B Wing, pilots. From left to right are: Gordon L. Young, Richard P. Sulzbach, Jack A. Savage, Thomas E. Green, Warren G. Nelson, and Don A. Oldis. (*McCallum collection*)

Squadron joined the wing. These pilots would be split among the three squadrons of the 20th (55th, 77th, and 79th Fighter-Bomber Squadrons). The 20 174th squadron pilots, along with the other 82 pilots of the 20th Fighter-Bomber Wing trained in high-altitude dive bombing at Langley (this technique would be replaced with the Low-Altitude Bombing System, or LABS, in 1953), as well as learning to fly on instruments in all kinds of weather. They went to the Kirkland AFB headquarters of the Special Weapons Center, and nearby Sandia Base in New Mexico for two weeks of nuclear weapons training. During their training in the U.S., and while flying in Europe after that, they never flew with the Mark 7 bomb, instead with the T-63 "nuclear shape."

The Wing left Langley May 22nd for their flight across the Atlantic for England. They arrived at Wethersfield, in Essex, England, on June 1, 1952. Because of crowded conditions on that airfield, the 79th Fighter-Bomber Squadron moved to RAF Bentwaters in Suffolk, England, that same day.

From their English bases, the squadrons of the 20th Fighter-Bomber Wing took up Victor Alert, which was nuclear-armed tactical fighters ready to respond to Soviet aggression (this was also known as Quick-Reaction Alert, or QRA). From these bases, the American airmen would fly along the Iron Curtain in a show of force. At times they would leave their bases in England and operate out of air fields in Germany for a week or so.

As 1952 approached its conclusion, in mid-November, the 174th Fighter-Bomber Squadron pilots in the 20th Fighter-Bomber Wing started rotating back to where they would be discharged, but not all of them. Some remained for an extended period, while others chose to remain in the Air Force.

Taking off for another mission of deterrence through nuclear strength. The 20th did not carry the Mark 7 bomb; they would carry the training "shape." (*National Museum of the USAF*)

Chapter 5

Starting Over

January 1, 1953, the 174th Fighter-Bomber Squadron was now part of the Iowa Air National Guard again. But there was not much more. What they came back to from their active duty was nothing like what they left. The large hangar and many facilities they left when going on active duty were taken over by the Air Force. What they got upon return were three small buildings in total that were part of the airport (city-owned) and not the air base. They had no aircraft, as the F-84Bs they flew out of Sioux City when going active were taken away and given to other Air Force units. The F-51Ds that replaced their jets stayed at Alexandria AFB in Louisiana and equipped another squadron. And on this date there were no personnel assigned to the squadron; by the 5th there were five pilot trainees.

Captain Donald W. Forney had been supply officer when the 174th was called to duty. Like most of the pilots, Captain Forney was stripped from the squadron and sent to another squadron. In his case he was sent to Korea, where he flew C-47 transports. He received the Air Medal for the missions he flew between March 6, 1952, and January 1, 1953. Forney

Sioux City Flying Service was a fixed base operator at Sioux City Municipal Airport. While the 174th Fighter-Bomber Squadron was on active duty, the USAF took over their large hangar and other facilities. When the 174th returned to Sioux City in January 1953, one of the few buildings that was allocated to them was this smaller hangar which was no longer in use by the fixed base operator. (*McCallum photo*)

Captain Donald W. Forney had been the 174th's supply officer prior to mobilization. As with most of the squadron's original pilots, he too was separated from his squadron. In his case he was sent to Korea, where he flew C-47s. He returned to the U.S. January 27th and became the 174th's new commanding officer the following day. (*174th FBS/McCallum collection*)

The F-51Ds that the 174th received as replacements for their F-84Bs went to an active duty unit when the 174th was returned to state control. They would be equipped for a third time with the F-51D, though only for a short time. They would also receive a number of T-6s. (*McCallum photo*)

returned to the U.S. in January, joined up with his old guard unit, and on January 28th was appointed commanding officer.

Rebuilding the squadron would take time, about two years Captain Forney thought. By March 15th, 10 officers (all pilots) and 156 enlisted men had returned to the squadron, and they had received two T-6 trainers. Within a week they received their first operational aircraft, an F-51D. More T-6 trainers, a C-47 transport, and additional F-51Ds would be received.

The F-51D would only be an interim aircraft for the squadron, and for the 132nd Fighter-Bomber Wing. By the summer of 1953, they knew they would soon be receiving Lockheed F-80 Shooting Star fighters. As in the past, their new mounts arrived somewhat later than expected. In mid-July, the 132nd Fighter-Bomber Wing/124th Fighter-Bomber

Early pilots in the re-established 174th Fighter-Bomber Squadron: Lieutenants Rocky, Oldis, and Sulzbach. (*174th FBS/ McCallum collection*)

Awaiting the arrival of their F-51 fighters. At first they only had these T-6s. (*McCallum photo*)

Squadron, based at Des Moines, received two F-80s and a T-33 trainer, while the 174th Fighter-Bomber Squadron in Sioux City received one F-80.

To prepare the Wing and its three squadrons for the F-80s, the 3497th Mobile Training Detachment from Chanute AFB, Illinois, along with nine instructors, set up a training facility in the Air National Guard hangar at Des Moines Municipal Airport. The training was carried out through July and August. The pilots of the 174th would fly to Des Moines on Sunday and Wednesday evenings for an abbreviated mechanics course to learn the fundamentals. A two week course was conducted for the mechanics. These courses included airframe, engine, and component operation and maintenance, in which mockups and other visual aids were used. The classroom work was followed up with hands-on tasks using the F-80s then on base. The T-33 at Des Moines was primarily for the Wing and the 124th Fighter-Bomber Squadron. Another T-33 was expected in August, which would be shared by both the 173rd (Lincoln, Nebraska) and 174th Fighter-Bomber Squadrons (Sioux City, Iowa). Each pilot would have ten hours of dual time with an instructor in the T-33 prior to soloing in an F-80.

It would take the month of August for the 174th to receive its full complement of F-80s, distributed in three increments throughout the month. Most of their aircraft would be F-80A models, along with a few F-80B models. By mid-month, eight of the squadron pilots were jet qualified and three more were expected to be qualified by month end. The month ended with a bang. An Air Force inspection team arrived from 10th Air Force headquarters, Selfridge AFB, Michigan. This annual inspection is a multi-day affair, in which unit records, equipment, personnel, maintenance, supply, and training are examined. This inspection is accomplished for

The F-51s at the 174th did not last long, as they received their first F-80A in mid-July 1953. In preparation for their jets, the pilots went to a jet transition course held at Des Moines, Iowa. Here, from left to right, are pilots Capt. Lyle K. Steely, Jr., Capt. Don A. Oldis, Maj. Donald W. Forney, Lt. Burton L. Rocky, and 1st Lt. Donald J. Love. (*174th FBS/McCallum collection*)

The Des Moines jet school was not just for the pilots. Here maintenance personnel are attending jet engine class. (*174th FBS/ McCallum collection*)

every Air Guard unit to insure that every facet of their operation meets Air Force requirements. There are only two grades: satisfactory and unsatisfactory. An unsatisfactory rating could jeopardize their federal recognition. This was the first inspection since coming back to state control. The squadron passed the inspection. Major Forney commented at the conclusion of the inspection that the inspection team was "particularly elated" over the units' training program and the condition of its aircraft, with special emphasis on safety factors.

The 174th held an open house and air show in mid-November, what today would be called a "community outreach" program—and as a

Along with the change from propeller-driven fighters to jet-propelled fighters, there was also a change to jet trainer aircraft. Pictured here is one of the squadron's T-33s. (*McCallum photo*)

recruiting effort. With four of their recently-arrived F-80s, they demonstrated formation flying, aerial tactics used in combat in Korea, made mock strafing runs, and simulated dive bombing attacks on the air base. Their T-33 performed acrobatics—always a crowd pleaser—and three of their T-6s made low level flights over the base. Part of the display in their hangar was a partially disassembled F-80, as well as an F-84.

The 173rd Fighter-Bomber Squadron from Lincoln, Nebraska, suffered a couple of fatal accidents in their F-80A aircraft. The first occurred in December 1953 near Crete, Nebraska, killing pilot Captain Fritz Craig. Some six weeks later, on January 24, 1954, Lt. Alden Ike was killed when his F-80 crashed shortly after takeoff near a nearby farm house. Two days later, it was announced that squadron commander Lt. Col. Fred H. Bailey, Jr. had grounded all of the squadron's F-80s. An investigation showed that the aircraft crashed because of a defective turbine wheel in the engine, causing control surface cables to be cut. These aircraft did not have ejection seats, which led to both pilots perishing. On February 9th, Iowa Air National Guard Headquarters grounded all F-80s for inspection.

On March 5th, it was announced that the F-80s of the 174th would resume flying as soon as inspections were completed, but not operationally. Major Forney stated that all of the 174th's F-80s would be sent to Lockheed Air Service, Inc., a division of Lockheed Aircraft Company in Burbank, California, for upgrades in April (actual date was May 13th). The upgrade would modify over 200 F-80As and F-80Bs throughout the Air National Guard. The modifications included newer and larger engines and the latest radio equipment and ejection seats, according to Iowa Adjutant General Major General Fred Tandy. With the upgrades, the F-80As and Bs that were modified

Base Operations in 1953. Pictured here are pilots 1st Lt. Alfred C. Grier, 1st Lt. Burton L. Rocky, 1st Lt. Richard C. Nurre, Capt. Richard P. Sulzbach, Capt. Don A. Oldis, Capt. Warren G. Nelson, Capt. Lyle K. Steely, Jr., and Capt. Elmo A. Solberg. (*174th FBS/ McCallum collection*)

into partial F-80C configuration were redesignated F-80C-11-LO and F-80C-12-LO, respectively. The F-80C-11-LO received the more powerful J33-A-35 engine, ejector seat using an M-5 catapult and M-3 actuator, provision for an AN/ARC-27 command radio, and the C-model tip tank. The F-80C-12-LO had a similar modification. Most of the 174th's aircraft became the F-80C-11-LO version of the Shooting Star, along with a few F-80C-12-LO and F-80A models.

The squadron received an additional assignment as 1954 started; they were to have the dual mission of ground support and air defense. In late February, the USAF notified the squadron that a squadron insignia had been approved. Apparently, the squadron had been working on one from their activation in December 1946, and finally submitted one that the USAF felt was appropriate and met their requirements. It was designed by Major Bert L. Goulait, the USAF air instructor assigned to the 174th.

When Air Guard units were called up for the Korean War, they had just recently restructured to match closer to the USAF combat wing structure. This restructuring brought about increased manning requirements. But the Air Guard hadn't been able to reach the previous manning level. Other reserve forces had similar problems. The 174th had its own struggles in reaching full manning. To assist all reserve branches in Sioux City, it was announced in May that the Sioux City (Iowa) Reserve Forces Committee had been formed to aid young men in planning their military service. Iowa Army and Air

Some of the F-80As and F-80Bs assigned on the flight line at Sioux City in January 1954. Accidents that past December, and later in January, would ground these aircraft. They would be sent to Lockheed in California and updated to F-80C configurations. (*McCallum photo*)

National Guard, Army Reserve, Naval Reserve, Marine Corps Reserve, and Air Force Reserve had representatives on the committee. Major Forney represented the Air National Guard.

In the 1950s, the threat of the Soviet Union striking the United States with an H-bomb seemed quite possible. One of the precautions to protect the American public from such danger was an exercise called Operation Alert. The U.S. Federal Civil Defense Agency initiated this exercise in June 1954, and held it as an annual event until 1961. The initial exercise was held between June 14 and 15, 1954. In this exercise, military defense forces, including the 174th Fighter-Bomber Squadron, and the civilian populace in major cities would react as if radar or ground observers had detected an aggressor force coming their way. Air raid sirens would go off, and the citizens were required to take cover for fifteen minutes. Military, civil defense, law enforcement, and other emergency personnel would check procedures and communications equipment under simulated attack circumstances.

The next month, an invasion was in the making when, on July 9, 1954, an armada of heavy bombers assembled in the area of the North Pole, ready for their charge to the military, industrial, and populated areas of Canada and the United States. To disrupt the defense forces of the United States and Canada, saboteurs were ready to spring into action. Fortunately, the aggressor's bomber fleet was USAF Strategic Air Command B-36s and B-47s. This was Operation Check Point. This exercise was under the command of General Benjamin W. Chidlau, commander of the USAF Air Defense Command in Colorado Springs, Colorado, and Air Vice Marshal

In early 1954, the 174th had the air defense mission added to their fighter-bomber mission, though they would not be designated a fighter-interceptor squadron until July 1955. (*McCallum photo*)

A. L. James, commander of the RCAF's Air Defense Command in Quebec, Canada.

A number of organizations in the Sioux City area were to participate. Intercepting the aggressor bombers were the USAF's 14th and 87th Fighter-Interceptor Squadrons stationed at the Sioux City Air Base, along with Iowa Air National Guard's 174th Fighter-Bomber Squadron. The Air Base, commanded by Colonel John A. Carey, had the added task of protecting the base from saboteurs. Being on the lookout for low flying hostile aircraft were the Ground Observer Corps volunteers manning 12 observer posts in Woodbury County—where Sioux City is located—lead by Civil Defense director Gordon C. Hollar.

Air Defense Command alerted the Sioux City units on the morning of July 9th that the exercise would take place sometime that month. That afternoon, the base was put on partial alert, with tighter restrictions being imposed around the base. At 7 o'clock that evening, the Ground Observer Corps volunteers were alerted and manned their posts. In Sioux City the post was on top of the Warrior hotel. The Observer Corps worked via phone with the air defense filter center in Omaha, Nebraska.

A few hours after midnight, in the early hours of July 10th, the first intercepts were made. From then on and into the morning of July 11th, the air and ground defenders were kept quite busy. The fighter squadrons not only did a lot of flying as part of the exercise, but they had to remain ready and capable of performing their real life mission should a real invasion be attempted. The purpose of this exercise was to evaluate the defense forces and identify areas that needed improvement. Though the results were classified, Colonel Carey stated

A pair of F-80s are scrambled on an air defense intercept mission. *(174th FBS/McCallum collection)*

that the intercepts were satisfactory and that the saboteurs were thwarted.

The Air Guard in Sioux City needed more facilities than the hangar and few small city-owned buildings they had. In July 1954, discussions between the Sioux City, Iowa, Adjutant General's office, National Guard Bureau in Washington, D.C., and U.S. property and dispersing officer began. The USAF had taken over the Guard's pre-Korean War area and more. According to original contractual arrangements between the U.S. government and the city at the end of World War II, the Air Force had the option to lease back some of what had been the Army Air Base. Now the Air Guard desired to gain some of the USAF property that was under its lease agreement with the city to become Air Guard-leased property on which a large hangar was to be constructed.

The U.S. Federal Civil Defense Agency held an air raid test exercise in mid-June. Apparently all did not go as smoothly as desired, so on December 8th, Operation Smoothout, a night exercise, was held to "smooth out" weaknesses found in the June effort. This test was for Air Defense Region 4, an eight-state area including Iowa. Iowa participated from 2 a.m. to 10 p.m., and it would start when air raid sirens went off in all 99 Iowa counties. Participating were Air National Guard units from Sioux City; Des Moines; Sioux Falls, South Dakota; Peoria, Illinois; and St. Joseph, Missouri, as well as naval reserve units from Lincoln, Nebraska; Minneapolis,

Sioux City Municipal Airport/Air National Guard Base in November 1954. (*174th FBS/McCallum collection*)

This Sioux City delegation is on its way to Washington, D.C., to confer with Air Force, National Guard, and Civil Aviation Administration (CAA, the predecessor of today's FAA) concerning acquiring Sioux City Air Base land from the Air Force on which to build permanent facilities for the 174th Fighter-Bomber Squadron. Pictured from left to right are: Major Donald W. Forney, 174th commanding officer; Richard W. Wolf, airport manager; W. B. Boucher, CAA representative; Paul V. Roberts, Public Works Administration; George W. Young, Sioux City mayor; and Robert M. Hoisington, city manager. (*174th FBS/McCallum collection*)

Minnesota; and Ottumwa, Iowa; besides Ground Observer Corps volunteers, Civil Air Patrol (their first time in a night exercise), USAF air defense units, and others.

The National Guard Bureau, under the command of Major General Edgar E. Erickson, planned a nationwide Air and Army National Guard mobilization test called Operation Minuteman in April 1955. To avoid panic among the American citizenry, announcement of the upcoming mobilization test was announced in the nation's newspapers in early April, but the date was kept secret. At 6 o'clock in the evening, April 21, 1955, Operation Minuteman was put into action. Phone calls, as well as radio and television announcements, alerted guardsmen to report for duty. The Army National Guard troops stationed in Sioux City reported to their Armory, and the 174th Fighter-Bomber Squadron of the Air National

On July 1, 1955, the 174th was redesignated Fighter-Interceptor. Here one of their F-80Cs is refueled prior to flight operations. (*174th FIS/McCallum collection*)

Guard reported to the Air Base. The 174th Fighter-Bomber Squadron, now with a fleet of 15 F-80s and about 400 personnel, had their first F-80 in the air within minutes. Soon others would either be in the air, or on alert and ready to takeoff on command. This was the largest peace-time operation attempted up to that time. At the conclusion of the operation, General Erickson felt that the guard's performance gave "conclusive proof" that they could assemble in a rapid, efficient manner.

In 1954, a shift in the Air Guard mission to continental air defense started. In February 1955, the 174th Fighter-Bomber Squadron was alerted that they would become a fighter-interceptor squadron. They were notified of the change May 23rd, and that it would be effective July 1st. This change included

Checking the guns and readying for flight. This F-80C-11 is one of the F-80As that was sent to Lockheed in Burbank, California, for upgrading. (*174th FBS/McCallum collection*)

This F-84B was delivered to the 174th Fighter-Interceptor Squadron in August 1955 to aid in the transition effort. Note that this F-84B has been retrofitted with an F-84E canopy. (*174th FIS/ McCallum collection*)

the 132nd Wing, as well as the 124th and 173rd Squadrons. The 174th Fighter-Interceptor Squadron was also informed that their Lockheed F-80Cs would soon be replaced by the Republic F-84E Thunderjet. In the same manner that ground school training was arranged in the 1953 transition to the F-80C, the same training would take place for pilots and maintenance troops converting to the F-84E.

To help in the transition training, the squadron received an F-84B and an early-block F-84E in August. The F-84B was unique, in that it had been assigned to the 174th in 1950 when they transitioned from F-51Ds to the F-84B. By December, they received a late-model F-84E for the transition training. One of the F-84s was partially disassembled and used for pilot indoctrination and maintenance training.

At the annual Air National Guard gunnery meet at Boise, Idaho, the 132nd Fighter-Interceptor Wing of the Iowa/Nebraska Air National Guard was declared the winner. Captain Gordon Young of the 174th placed second in individual score, only two points behind the first place finisher.

Air Defense Command in Colorado Springs conducted two exercises in the last quarter of 1955. The first occurred on October 25th and was called Operation Stop Watch. Seventy Air National Guard fighter-interceptor squadrons, including the 174th, participated in the exercise. The purpose of the exercise was to determine the Air Guard's response

Crew Chief Earl Duvall assists pilot Gordon Young to prepare for the day's flight. In the background is an F-84C taxiing by. This aircraft, along with an F-84B, was assigned to the 174th FIS to assist in the conversion from F-80Cs to F-84Es. (*174th FIS/McCallum collection*)

Sioux City ANG Base flight ramp in August 1955. Aircraft in the hangar and on the ramp include T-6s, F-80s, T-33s, and F-84s. (*174th FIS/McCallum collection*)

Cadets Douglas E. Burr (right) and Ronald F. Lenagh (left) inspect an F-84E in the Sioux City ANG hangar in December 1955. (*174th FIS/McCallum collection*)

Major Donald W. Forney gives a briefing in preparation for Operation Stop Watch. (*174th FIS/McCallum collection*)

time to an alert under winter conditions. The 174th was notified of the alert at 7:45 a.m. The first aircraft were in the air by 8:25 a.m., and within an hour of being notified of the alert, half of the squadron's aircraft were airborne. Major Forney, squadron commander, stated that the 174th performed successfully. Nationally, 50 percent of the 73 Air Guard fighter squadrons that participated were deemed combat ready within two hours of notification, according to Air Defense Command headquarters.

The second occurred on December 6th and was called Operation Crackerjack. This was a much larger exercise, which included USAF, Air Force Reserve, Air National Guard, civil defense volunteers, and Canadian forces. This exercise

A pair of 174th FIS F-80s scramble as part of Operation Stop Watch. The purpose of this exercise was to evaluate Air National Guard units on their response time to alerts called in winter conditions. (*174th FIS/ McCallum collection*)

concerned the nation's capability of repelling an airborne attack. SAC played the part of the attacking forces, which included the use of B-36 and B-47 bombers. Though it was originally estimated that the alert would be for a number of days, it wound up lasting 14 hours. At Sioux City Air Base, the USAF's 13th and 14th Fighter-Interceptor Squadrons (flying F-86D interceptors) stood on alert during the exercise; the 174th Fighter-Interceptor Squadron of the Iowa Air National Guard, whose planes did not have airborne intercept radar, stood alert only during daylight hours.

Since returning from active duty in January 1953, the Air Guard needed to obtain more land and facilities, including a larger hangar. Discussions started in July 1954 with city, Guard, and Air Force representatives. Word was received in April 1955 that the 174th would get 40 acres at the air base, and on November 15th, a new air base pact was signed which provided the squadron with a site for their proposed installation. On May 4, 1956, bids were opened for their new facilities. W. A. Klinger Co. of Sioux City was awarded the contract, which included a large hangar measuring 212 feet by 203 feet, supply facility, ammunition storage facility, motor pool, paint and dope storage facility, aircraft parking apron, wash rack, and utilities-driveway-parking area, as well as grading space, drainage, and security fence.

The 174th Fighter-Interceptor Squadron excelled in their training in 1956. They received the coveted

Guard duty on the Sioux City flight line in support of Operation Crackerjack in December 1955. (*174th FIS/McCallum collection*)

Air National Guard summer camp at Casper, Wyoming. (*174th FIS/McCallum collection*)

Spaatz Trophy and the Air Force Association Award as the outstanding Air National Guard squadron in the country, among the many other accolades received that year. At their annual field training at Casper, Wyoming, in 1956, the 174th won the Gwinn Trophy as the top performing squadron in training. Captain Lyle Steely, 174th Operations Officer, took top score for air-to-air gunnery. A couple of months later, the 132nd Fighter-Interceptor Wing participated in the USAF World-Wide Gunnery meet at Nellis AFB, Nevada. Their team of four pilots included pilot Captain Gordon L. Young of the 174th, along with support personnel from the squadron. This team finished fourth among all the units competing.

Air Force Association award given to the 174th Fighter-Interceptor Squadron in 1956. (*174th FIS/McCallum collection*)

All practice exercises, sometimes called "operations," are not large scale, or even statewide. Major Forney of the 174th Fighter-Interceptor Squadron thought that the New Year holiday weekend would be an appropriate time. At around noon on Saturday, December 29, 1956, he called a four-hour alert. Not only did some squadron members live over 160 miles away, there were also the holiday vacations. By phone, radio, and television the word went out. In less than an hour the first fighter was airborne. Thirteen pilots reported in within the first hour. The aggressors were two T-33 trainers. When it was over, each pilot flew at least one intercept. In one case, Major Gale Stevens landed his fighter and it was refueled, reloaded with ammunition and oxygen, serviced, and airborne with a relief pilot within 10 minutes! The outcome was that 83 percent of the officers and over 65 percent of the airmen responded to the alert.

Spaatz Trophy awarded to the 174th Fighter-Interceptor Squadron in 1956. (*174th FIS/McCallum collection.*

1957 started with great expectations on the part of the 132nd Fighter-Interceptor Wing (Des Moines, Iowa) and its three squadrons: the 124th (Des Moines), the 173rd (Lincoln, Nebraska), and the 174th (Sioux City, Iowa). As fighter-interceptor squadrons, they expected to be equipped with airborne intercept radar-carrying fighters. The 173rd Fighter-Interceptor Squadron began receiving North American F-86D Sabre in January. By March, Lt. Col. Roger W. Gilbert, wing commander of the 132nd, stated that he expected the 124th and 174th squadrons would soon also be equipped with the Sabre. Planning for simulator training buildings and rocket storage facilities at Sioux City and Des Moines was in the works. That same month, Major Forney of the 174th announced that his squadron had been allocated 25 F-86D all-weather interceptors.

How does the Marine Hymn go—From the halls of Montezuma to the shores of the Missouri? That's how it was on a June Sunday in 1957, when, in a six-hour ground combat exercise, Marine reservists and 174th Air Guardsmen went from the sandy banks of the Missouri to a group of farm buildings (simulating an enemy radar station) manned by opposition forces (naval reservists). It was quite an experience for the Air Guardsmen, especially the officer that stumbled over a tripwire and both he and his M-1 rifle went down into the mud.

The 174th's C.O. called an alert December 29, 1956. This was an annual event for many years. On four-hour alert duty is pilot Capt. James Hanlon and crew chief Earl Duvall. (*174th FIS/ McCallum collection*)

For the first years of existence, the 174th had a very large hangar in which they could store most of their aircraft, along with many other buildings to support personnel, operations, and support functions. When they returned from the Korean call up, they found all had been taken over by others, and what they were given was not adequate. From negotiations, to design, to bidding, to building, they once again had brand new and very adequate facilities. On August 9, 1957, the process of moving in started. On September 22nd, they dedicated their new facility and held an open house in celebration. The total cost of the project was $1,300,000.

As part of their air defense mission, the 174th Fighter-Interceptor Squadron participated in

F-86Ds like the ones assigned to the 173rd Fighter-Interceptor Squadron and expected for a while by the 174th. (*USAF*)

First operational F-84E received by the 174th Fighter-Interceptor Squadron on May 11, 1956. (*174th FIS/McCallum collection*)

performing alert duty in local practice alerts and Air Force/Air Guard exercises. These included four-hour alerts showing that the squadron was ready to take off and defend the greater Sioux City area. To prove their readiness, the 174th took part in a practice alert November 16, 1957. They were found to be mission capable, and Sioux City was safe from a Soviet bomber threat.

As Major Forney did last December, he called another alert in 1958. This time it was on Saturday, November 16th. The call went out by telephone, radio, and television announcement. The 450 members lived in the four states surrounding Sioux City. One member flew a private plane owned by

Checking the guns. An F-84E of the 174th FIS is readied by armament troops while the pilot patiently awaits his opportunity to perform his assigned mission. (*174th FIS/McCallum collection*)

Iowa's 174th Fighter-Interceptor Squadron had joint summer training at Casper, Wyoming, in 1956 with Nebraska's 173rd Fighter-Interceptor Squadron. (*174th FIS/McCallum collection*)

the company he worked for and picked up other members on his way to Sioux City. Within an hour of the alert there were sufficient pilots and support personnel to launch all of the squadron's tactical aircraft. Within two hours of the alert, 77 percent of the personnel had reported in. Their performance in this type of alert counted in the decision of which squadron would win the Spaatz Trophy each year. Major Forney was quite pleased with the outcome of the alert and called it "gratifying."

The 174th Fighter-Interceptor Squadron was one of 118 Air Guard units that took proficiency tests in 1957. They ranked fifth.

Chapter 6

Eye in the Sky

1958 started off with quite a surprise for the 174th Fighter-Interceptor Squadron. They had performed well in their annual federal inspections, at annual Air Guard summer training, in gunnery, and had won a number of awards, including the prestigious Spaatz Trophy. They expected to be equipped with the North American F-86D intercept radar-equipped fighter. In a letter from the National Guard Bureau dated January 13th, the squadron was notified that as of January 15th they were removed from the 132nd Fighter-Interceptor Wing, headquartered in Des Moines, Iowa, and assigned to the 118th Tactical Reconnaissance Wing headquartered in Nashville, Tennessee. "What happened?" they probably asked. Air Defense Command had been quite skeptical about Air National Guard's capability to maintain and effectively operate "complicated missile-firing fighters."

The annual two-week summer training would change from Casper, Wyoming, to Gulfport, Mississippi. The 174th's C.O., Major Donald W. Forney, flew down to Gulfport in late January to meet with personnel there and returned on Monday, February 3rd. Two days after his arrival back in Iowa, Forney and Iowa's Adjutant General, Major General Fred C. Tandy, announced the squadron's change in mission, command, and aircraft. They would be re-equipped with the Republic RF-84F Thunderflash, and they would be redesignated a tactical reconnaissance squadron on April 10th.

When Major Forney returned from Gulfport on Monday, he found that he had another concern besides the change in mission facing him. That Sunday, 2nd Lt. Richard O. Wikert was in the final phase of his pre-takeoff check when the engine apparently caught fire. Lt. Wikert got out of the F-84E unscathed, but Robert Conley, a civilian member of the air base fire department, inhaled the fumes from the bromochloromethane used to extinguish the fire and ended up in Sioux City's Methodist Hospital; he was reported in good condition. The F-84E was described as a near total loss. Major Forney stated the damaged plane, as well as the squadron's other aircraft, would be scrapped.

Initial transition efforts started to move along rapidly. In mid-February, Major Forney and some of his staff went to Nashville to meet with 118th Tactical Reconnaissance Group and Wing personnel concerning mission and training at Sioux City for the squadron as well as at the two-week Gulfport effort, and squadron-group-wing interface. The squadron received its first RF-84F on March 18th and

In preparation for the squadron's change to RF-84Fs, Major Forney and some of his staff went to the 118th Tactical Reconnaissance Wing headquarters in Nashville, Tennessee, in February 1958. (*174th FIS/McCallum collection*)

The first RF-84F landed at Sioux City March 18, 1958. It drew the attention of 174th pilots and crew chiefs. Present in the crowd is Capt. William Hart, the squadron maintenance officer, who accepted the plane for the 174th TRS from Lt. W. R. Kemp, who had just flown the plane in from Hill AFB, Utah. (*174th FIS/McCallum collection*)

To assist in the transition from F-84Es to the RF-84F tactical photo recon aircraft, the 174th was assigned six F-84F fighter version of the swept-wing Republic aircraft. The first three F-84Fs arrived May 2, 1958. (*174th TRS/McCallum collection*)

three of six F-84Fs on May 2nd. The latter aircraft would be assigned to the 174th for 1958, as their sole purpose was in the transition effort. In mid-April, the Air Force sent a Mobile Training Detachment to Sioux City to assist the squadron in learning about their new aircraft, photographic equipment, film processing, photo intelligence, etc. The detachment consisted of some 20 specialists, around 30 crates of training aids and mockups, and all-day classes for six weeks. The Mobile Training Detachment completed their work at Sioux City on May 23rd, and went to Gulfport, Mississippi, where they would work with the squadron during their summer training between June 15th and 29th. Also, by May 24th, the squadron had six of their RF-84Fs, with the remaining 12 expected prior to leaving for Gulfport.

Apparently morale was low in the squadron when the change of mission first came down from headquarters. By the time they went to Gulfport, they had started to warm to their new mission. The troops started to refer to their new mission as "Kill 'Em with 'Fillum'." The squadron took 11 of their aircraft—a mixture of F-84Fs and RF-84F—to their June annual training camp. Here all put their new tasks into action: JATO takeoffs, filming targets, processing and interpreting the film, and maintenance of cameras and aircraft were practiced.

Tensions broke out in the Middle East in the summer of 1958 (these tensions dated back to 1956 and the Suez Crisis). On one side were the pro-Western Lebanese Christians and the effect of the pro-western Baghdad Pact. On the other

The photo lab was no longer only responsible for taking pictures and developing them. Here 174th personnel are learning how to develop the film from their RF-84F cameras during their two week summer training at Gulfport, Mississippi. (174th TRS/McCallum collection)

At first, the 174th Tactical Reconnaissance Squadron did not have the appropriate equipment for drying their film, so they made do with what they had. Here they are using the chairs of a classroom to drape their film over. (*174th TRS/McCallum collection*)

side were the United Arab Republic (Egypt and Syria), along with general Arab nationalism and Lebanese Muslims. On July 14th, the pro-Western government in Iraq was toppled. The following day, U.S. President Dwight D. Eisenhower authorized Operation Blue Bat. Blue Bat was the first application of the Eisenhower Doctrine. This was followed on the 17th by Air Defense Command calling an alert. Sioux City Air Base and its interceptors were included in the alert, but the 174th, now a tactical reconnaissance squadron, did not do much, to the dismay of some.

The 174th was used to the annual alerts called by their commander to measure their response time and readiness. When Major Forney called one on October 18th, instead of taking to the air to intercept incoming hostiles, they mounted their speedy photo planes. This time their mission was to take aerial photos of distant cities, dams, power plants, and railroad yards. Both response to the call to report in (70 per cent within the first two hours) and

Installing a jet assist to (JATO) unit to one of the F-84Fs. (174th TRS/McCallum collection)

JATO takeoff. (*174th TRS/McCallum collection*)

One of the squadron's F-84F Thunderstreaks readies for takeoff. (*174th TRS/McCallum collection*)

Sandra "Sandy" Olson was Miss Iowa in 1958. Here she pays a visit to the Sioux City Air Guard in the summer of that year. (174th TRS/McCallum collection)

An RF-84F of the 174th TRS flies over Sioux City in the late 1950s or early 1960s. Below is the meandering Floyd River. The Floyd had a history of overflowing and causing disaster, with 1953 being one of the worst. In the 1960s, that part of the Floyd that went through Sioux City was straightened out and flood control enhancements were incorporated. (*174th TRS/McCallum collection*)

performing their intelligence mission were "highly successful," according to Major Forney.

The year ended in near tragedy. Sgt. Earl Duvall was working around one of the RF-84Fs, whose engine was running, and was ingested in the aircraft's air intake. Sergeant Duvall was taken to St. Vincent hospital, where X-rays fortunately showed no fractures; he had only suffered facial lacerations and abrasions. Duvall temporarily lost his sight, but regained it, and after recuperating was able to return to his Guard duties.

In late January, the 174th acted as host base for RF-84F aircraft and crews from Alabama, Arkansas, Mississippi, and Missouri. They were to act as the aggressors in an Air Defense Command tactical evaluation exercise. Their mission during January 24 and 25, 1959, was to attempt to penetrate pre-

On December 17, 1958, crew chief Sgt. Earl Duvall got too close to the intake of this RF-84F and was sucked into the inlet. (*174th TRS/ McCallum collection*)

determined air defense areas, one of which was Lincoln AFB, Nebraska. Though the results were classified, apparently, the Lincoln 173rd Fighter-Interceptor Squadron grumbled over the airwaves because of the many scrambles.

The USAF, like the Army Air Forces before them, had little use for the Air National Guard prior to the Korean call-up. The call-up found the Air Guard generally under-equipped, under-manned, under-trained, and quite far from being mission ready. Lack of funding was a large contributor to the problem. The states had an attitude of wanting to keep separate from federal control and direction. They resisted to the extent that, down at the technical manual level, the states did not necessarily follow what the Air Force provided. Things began to improve after the call-up and continued to improve over the years, though whenever budgets are tightened, the Air Force tends to minimize the Air Guard. And that continues today.

For three days in late April, the National Guard Bureau, in conjunction with Continental Air Command—who has USAF supervision responsibility over the Air Guard—as well as representatives from other USAF commands who would have Air Guard units assigned to them during an emergency held a conference at Ellington AFB, Texas. Attending were commanders and other representatives from Air Guard units representing all states, territories, and the District of Columbia. Representing the squadron were Major Donald W. Forney, C.O. of the 174th, along with Captain Gordon L. Young, the squadron's operations officer. The purpose of the conference was to improve combat readiness of Air National Guard units in conjunction with sharing their operational commitments with the USAF. Major elements affecting Air Guard combat readiness discussed at the conference included: Air Guard commanders needed to be combat ready in their assigned mission aircraft, or they needed to be replaced; the Air Guard needed more Century Series aircraft; and the Air Guard needed to share in Air Force missile programs and flying safety (which directly relates to combat readiness).

While Major Forney and Captain Young were attending the planning conference in Texas,

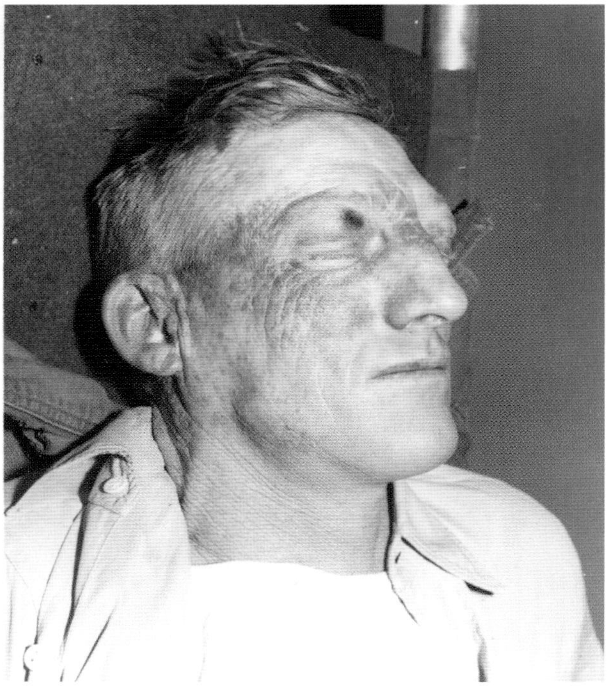

Sgt Duvall was taken to St. Vincent hospital in Sioux City, where X-ray inspection showed no fractures. As can be seen in the above photo, he suffered facial lacerations and abrasions. Though he was initially blinded by the incident, he quickly regained his sight. (*174th TRS/McCallum collection*)

Operation Eye-Opener was taking place. As so many of the exercises go, this was another test of American and Canadian air defenses. Six pilots from the 174th Tactical Reconnaissance Squadron, and many more from nine other squadrons coming from the far corners of the United States, took part in the exercise. The 174th flew to Newfoundland, Canada, and from there they would attempt to photograph important Canadian targets as defending forces attempted to fend them off. As usual the outcome was not published for security reasons, but the 117th Photo-Reconnaissance Squadron of the Kansas Air National Guard, who flew RB-57As, states in its history (actually the 190th ARW of today), "There is no point in telling the Soviet Union's Manned Bomber Command what their chances are."

A major joint Army-Air Force exercise called Dark Cloud-Pine Cone II (Dark Cloud being the Army name for the exercise and Pine Cone II the Air Force's) was held between May 23 and June 7, 1959; planning by participants took place in March and April. This two-week exercise was a rehearsal

Operation Eye-Opener consisted of 10 tactical reconnaissance squadrons attempting to photograph specific targets in parts of Canada while being challenged by defending aircraft. Three of the six 174th TRS pilots taking part in this operation are shown studying a map. They are, from left to right: Capt. Robert E. German, Capt. Lawrence J. Kennedy, Jr., and 2nd Lt. Gene J. Johnson. Also participating from the 174th are: 1st Lt. Neil L. Brunick, 1st Lt. Douglas E. Burr, and 2nd Lt. Roger J. Heisterkamp. (*174th TRS/ McCallum collection*)

for brush fire type of war. It was billed as the largest war game involving Air National Guard and Air Force Reserve forces since the Korean War, as well as Army troops (including the 82nd Airborne Division). Twenty-five Air Guard fighter and reconnaissance squadrons and 15 Air Reserve troop carrier wings were contributing personnel, aircraft, and support. Because of the length of the exercise, and that it would not count towards the annual two-week training period required for guardsmen and reservists, those that volunteered to participate were put on active duty for this time period.

The actual maneuvers took place some 150 miles from Ft. Bragg, North Carolina. Air operations were staged out of Congaree ANG Base and Donaldson AFB South Carolina, Pope AFB and Seymour-Johnson AFB North Carolina, and Kanawha Airport, West Virginia. The provisional reconnaissance wing, designated Cocoa, was made up of RF-84F aircraft, pilots, and support personnel from ten Air Guard squadrons. Their mission was to photograph troop concentrations, supply depots, and enemy movement. For the first week of the exercise, the 174th led the reconnaissance wing. Major

RB-57A of the 117th Photo-Reconnaissance Squadron of the Kansas Air National Guard. (190th ARW)

Forney was commander; Captains Warren Nelson, Gordon Young, and Lawrence Kennedy were flight leaders. Major James E. Hardwick, of Alabama's 160th Tactical Reconnaissance Squadron, was wing commander during the second week. They arrived only three days prior to commencement of the war games, which gave little time for the different members of the various ANG squadrons to get to know each other, much less get all the equipment ready and prepared to enter "combat."

The outcome for the Air Guard bode quite well. This was the first time since Korea that Air Guard officers filled top command and staff positions. At Congaree, the guardsmen operated in tents and in the open without the heavy gear they would normally have at their disposal. The reconnaissance wing processed 3,586 feet of aerial film and printed 5,760 photos. Major General Henry Viccellio, 10th Air Force commander and Deputy Director for Air in the exercise, stated that the Air Guard "performed exceptionally well." In regard to aircraft repair and maintenance, the Guard's performance was described as amazing, almost unbelievable.

Major General Earl T. Ricks was chief of the Air Force Division and deputy chief of the National Guard Bureau from 1951 until he died from illness in January 1954. To commemorate the late general, the Air Force Association inaugurated a race for Air National Guard fighters on July 24th of that year. The winner of the race was presented the Earl T. Ricks Memorial Trophy. In 1958, the Air Force Association incorporated a mission-specific aspect. That year, Air Guard fighter-interceptor units flying the North American F-86D were invited to participate. In this

Operation Pine Cone II took place in May and June 1959 in the North and South Carolina area. Here four pilots from the 174th TRS prepare their flight plan. They are, left to right: Capt. Warren G. Nelson, Major Donald W. Forney, Capt. Laurence J. Kennedy, Jr., and Capt. Gordon L. Young. (*174th TRS/McCallum collection*)

The Earl T. Ricks Memorial Trophy race in 1959 was a tactical reconnaissance affair. Capt. John J. Cottingham, the 174th's assistant operations officer (left), and 2nd Lt. Richard O. Wikert (right) were selected from the 174th to try out for the right to represent the squadron. Capt. Cottingham won the honor of flying the primary RF-84F and Lt. Wikert stood by with the backup should Cottingham have a problem. (*174th TRS/McCallum collection*)

The 174th TRS Ricks team. Capt. John J. Cottingham and 2nd Lt. Richard O. Wikert in the back row (left to right). In the front row, left to right, are the crew chiefs: MSgt Harold Andresen, TSgt Norman J. Moon, and TSgt Lloyd F. Donovan. (*174th TRS/ McCallum collection*)

competition, not only flying time was involved, but intercepts of T-33s had to be accomplished. The 173rd Fighter-Interceptor Squadron of the Nebraska Air Guard, stationed at Lincoln, won the trophy.

The 1959 competition was open to photo reconnaissance squadrons flying the Republic RF-84F. The 174th Tactical Reconnaissance Squadron, along with nine other squadrons, entered the competition. Two pilots were initially selected: Captain John J. Cottingham, the Assistant Operations Officer, and 2nd Lt. Richard O. Wikert. They both tested the squadron's stable of aircraft to determine which were the fastest. They then practiced the 850-mile course. Next, the ground crew went over both aircraft to insure all was functioning well, tuned them up for maximum performance, and polished them to a high sheen. In late August, it was announced that Captain Cottingham was the primary pilot, while Lt. Wikert and his aircraft would be standby, in case Cottingham had aircraft problems.

The race took place September 2nd, and was from Memphis, Tennessee, to Miami, Florida. It was timed to kick off the Air Force Association that year, which was being held in Miami. While making their speed run, the pilots had to photograph at least three of 10 targets. Two targets were mandatory: the state capitol in Tallahassee, Florida, and MacDill AFB, Tampa, Florida. To win the Ricks trophy, both the speed and clarity of their photos would be considered. The photo processing and evaluation was accomplished by the 165th Tactical Reconnaissance Squadron of the Kentucky Air Guard. The 117th Aircraft Control

Ricks Trophy Race—The Instructions. (*174th TRS/McCallum collection*)

Ricks Race—The Draw. (*174th TRS/McCallum collection*)

Ricks Race—The Drivers. (*174th TRS/McCallum collection*)

Capt. Cottingham in 174th TRS RF-84F "The City of Sioux City." (*174th TRS/McCallum collection*)

and Warning Flight of the Georgia Air Guard, using a mobile radar facility at Miami, provided in-flight support and "clocked in" each aircraft.

Clouds hindered the pilots, and unfortunately also 1st Lt. Robert G. Graham of the 105th Tactical Reconnaissance Squadron, Nashville, Tennessee. Though he clocked in at 580 miles per hour, two of his three photos were judged unacceptable. Captain Donald K. Reid of Michigan's 171st, whose average speed was 570 miles per hour, was awarded the Ricks Memorial Trophy. The 174th's Cottingham came in fourth in the speed phase at 550 miles per hour, but below fourth in the trophy standings. Besides the winner receiving the trophy, those that placed second, third, and fourth received special plaques at the Air Force Association convention.

The 174th was used to the annual federal inspections that they had passed. In September 1959 a new wrinkle was added, an Operational Readiness Test. Not only were all facets inspected, but they had to prove it to the Air Force. This five-day event was labeled an Operational Readiness Inspection, referred to even now as an ORI.

The 174th, as are all Air National Guard units, is always ready to assist in local, state, regional, and national emergencies. In the first half of 1960, the 174th was ready and able to assist. The Graham Clinic Pharmacy in Mitchell, South Dakota, found themselves in dire need of flu serum. The McKesson & Robins Drug Company in Sioux City was called by the clinic for emergency services. The 174th was then contacted for assistance, and within an hour the

A mission of mercy. TSgt Melvin Larson of the 174th TRS receives an emergency shipment of flu serum for Mitchell, South Dakota, from McKesson Robbins Drug Company's local manager, Mr. Eklad. Flying the 174th's C-47 are Major Don Oldis and Capt. James Hanlon. (*174th TRS/McCallum collection*)

vaccine was being handed to TSgt Melvin Larson in the doorway of the squadron's C-47, which was then flown to Mitchell by Major Don Oldis and Captain James Hanlon.

To this day the Missouri, Big Sioux, and Floyd rivers have flooded the tri-state area around Sioux City and beyond. In late March and early April 1960 it happened again. And once again the 174th was there to help. Sixty-four members of the squadron were called to active duty by the state for two days, but many others volunteered their assistance as need required. There were ample personnel in the squadron to help, as this year's Muster Day, an annual event used for recruiting, showed there

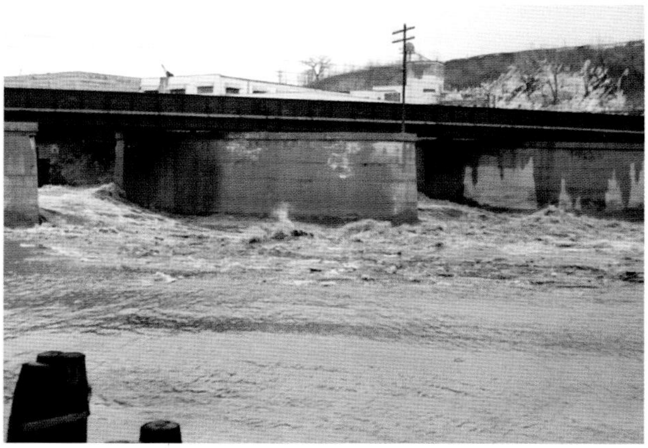

In 1960, the Missouri, Big Sioux, and Floyd rivers went over their banks and once again brought disaster to the Sioux City area. (*174th TRS/McCallum collection*)

Even the aid workers needed some well deserved rest. (*174th TRS/ McCallum collection*)

Providing comfort and supplies for those in need. (*174th TRS/ McCallum collection*)

Another practice alert. A pilot checks in at Sioux City Air National Guard base operations. (*174th TRS/McCallum collection*)

A 174th TRS pilot mounts his RF-84F during the practice alert, ready to fly to whatever target is assigned. (*174th TRS/McCallum collection*)

were no vacancies in the unit and those interested were put on a waiting list.

Whether being tested as defenders or testing the defenders, the 174th participated vigorously. This time three of the squadron pilots, along with their Air Force squadron adviser, Major James E. Beitzel, flew to Charleston AFB, South Carolina, and then on to Kindley AFB, Bermuda. Here 28 other Air National Guard pilots and their aircraft staged out in the last weekend of August. Not a new scenario to the 174th, this time it was Captain John J. Cottingham, 1st Lt. Jerry Edwards, and 1st Lt. Gene M. Johnson representing the squadron. The mission of the 32 Air Guardsmen was to test, and penetrate if possible, the air defenses of the southeastern seaboard of the United States. As usual, the results of this air defense exercise were not released and no incident reported. But a month later, Lt. Edwards did have a thriller. He was on his way back to Sioux City from the West Coast when he had a flameout over North Platte, Nebraska. He was able to get the engine restarted, but found he was getting low on fuel as he was approaching Norfolk, Nebraska. He landed at Norfolk's Karl Stefan Memorial Airport, but found they did not have the jet fuel he needed. Within a few hours a fuel tanker load of jet fuel arrived from Sioux City and he prepared to takeoff. Due to the somewhat short length of the runway, the local fire crew was ready to go into action if he did not make it. He did.

The 174th strived to show it was one of the best units in the Air National Guard. They had won many awards, the greatest being the Spaatz Trophy in 1954. Their winning streak continued with the 1960 Operational Readiness Inspection in August, when they flew twice the number of sorties as required and had a 94 percent in-commission rate of tactical aircraft. The crowning achievement was their being designated the top operationally ready RF-84F unit in the Air National Guard.

Artist SSgt Donald L. "Jake" Jacobson completes his mural in the 174th's snack bar. The mural depicts the different aircraft flown by the 174th since its inception. In 1962, Jacobson would update his painting by replacing the large RF-84F with an F-100C. (*174th TRS/McCallum collection*)

Home of the 174th Tactical Reconnaissance Squadron. (*174th TRS/McCallum collection*)

The last of the 174th's RF-84Fs can still be seen today, as it is part of the 185th Air Refueling Wing's display of aircraft on the base. (*McCallum photo*)

Chapter Seven

Prelude to Combat

In late 1960, the National Guard Bureau cited nine Air National Guard units as "top operational readiness" in type of aircraft and shared the trophy of the National Guard Association's U.S. The 174th Tactical Reconnaissance Squadron was awarded in the RF-84F tactical reconnaissance category. They were at the top of their game again, and again, they would have their aircraft and mission changed.

In January 1961, the wheels were put in motion. Near Denver, Colorado, the 120th Tactical Fighter Squadron (Special Delivery), stationed at Buckley ANG Base (home unit for the Air National Guard's famed Minutemen flight demonstration team), would be joined by the 174th Tactical Reconnaissance Squadron and Kansas' 127th Fighter-Interceptor Squadron to form the 140th Tactical Fighter Wing, also at Buckley ANG Base. All three squadrons would be equipped with North American F-100C Super Sabres later that year. Lt. Col. Don Forney, 174th commander, went to Denver in late January/early February to confer with 140th Tactical Fighter Wing commander, Col. Walter E. Williams, and his staff. Col. Williams, along with Kansas adjutant general Brig. Gen. Edward F. Fry, came to Sioux City in early February to meet with Lt. Col. Forney. Though undocumented, it is rumored that Forney had been asked earlier if he wanted to change to fighters or stay in tactical reconnaissance, and he jumped at the chance of getting into fighters again. In the February 5th issue of the *Sioux City Journal* newspaper, Forney stated that as of that date the 174th was a Tactical Fighter Squadron, and was under the 140th Tactical Fighter Wing.

174th Tactical Fighter Squadron (Special Delivery). (*174th TFS/ McCallum collection*)

By late March, major construction bids had been let in support of the new mission. This included a crash/fire station, an engine buildup shop, and vehicle parking facilities. Altogether, construction costs amounted to about $90,000. But apparently, for some reason, the February 5th announcement of the change was postponed until May 1st. Kansas' 127th became a Tactical Fighter Squadron (SD) on April 1st. With the new mission and aircraft, the 174th had to add 80 more officers and airmen to its rolls, bringing it to a total of 532 personnel.

Special Delivery in the unit's designation referred to the tactical use of nuclear weapons. These bombs would be delivered by the F-100C Super Sabres in a technique in which the pilot would come in at supersonic speed to a pre-

On April 15, 1961, 140th Tactical Fighter Wing commander, Col. Walter E. Williams, flew an F-100C to Sioux City to show the 174th what they had to look forward to. Pictured are, from the left: Lt. Col. Donald W. Forney, Col. Williams, Capt. John J. Cottingham, Major Warren G. Nelson, and Major William Hart. (*174th TFS/ McCallum collection*)

determined point, at which he would pull up into a vertical climb. When near the crest of the climb the bomb was automatically released. As it was released it continued upward, arched over, and then plummeted towards its target. In the meantime, the pilot had performed an Immelmann after the bomb was released from the aircraft and rushed off at top speed to avoid as much of the bomb blast as possible. The squadron had a head start in learning this technique. Major Gale D. V. Stevens, squadron operations officer, was the first pilot ever to drop a bomb (inert) using this method when he was stationed at Eglin AFB, Florida, in 1952.

Even with the delay in mission changeover, preparations proceeded. The 174th would be getting their 25 F-100Cs from the 36th Tactical Fighter Wing in Bitburg AB, Germany. To get a firsthand look at the aircraft they would be receiving, along with insight into the operations and maintenance of the aircraft, the National Guard Bureau arranged for Lt. Col. Don Forney to accompany Major General Ben I. Funk, commander of the San Bernardino (California) Air Material Area, on his European trip in his turboprop Boeing C-97J Stratofreighter. They flew via the Province of Newfoundland, the Islands of the Azores in the Atlantic, then to England, Germany, and Italy. While at Bitburg, Germany, Forney received counsel from the 36th Tactical Fighter Wing on his new mission, as well as such topics as maintenance and supply problems and possible solutions relating to the F-100C.

As a tactical fighter squadron, the 174th would now be under the command of the 140th Tactical Fighter Wing in Denver, Colorado. In June, this VIP team arrived at Sioux City to assist the 174th with this newest conversion of aircraft and mission. (*174th TFS/McCallum collection*)

The first F-100C arrived at Sioux City June 3, 1961. The squadron's F-100Cs were coming from the 36th Tactical Fighter Wing, based at Bitburg, Germany. (*174th TFS/McCallum collection*)

In July, an F-100 transition training team landed in Sioux City. (*174th TFS/McCallum collection*)

In early 1961, classroom training started for pilots, as well as maintenance and support personnel. Throughout the spring, 174th personnel traveled to both Denver and Wichita for instruction in their new mission and aircraft. Back in Sioux City, the 174th continued classroom instruction. The first F-100C arrived June 3rd, and from that point on-the-job training was conducted using this aircraft as the classroom. The standard 15-day summer training encampment is a time when all squadron members travel as a unit to a distant location from their home station to practice their military profession. Because of the squadron being totally consumed in converting from one mission and aircraft to another, the National Guard Bureau allowed the 174th to have a modified Texas Plan type of field training. In the Texas Plan type of training, the 174th was allowed to have continuous training throughout the summer, and squadron members would perform their required 15 days at the best time for them and their employers. The Air Force provided an F-100 Mobile Training Detachment throughout the 90-day period. For the pilots, the training consisted of six days of ground school and then five to seven hours of briefing before each mission. To ready the squadron for their new mission during this extended training period, support elements of the 174th and personnel of the Mobile Training Detachment were spending eight to 16 hours per day, seven days a week, to complete their training effort. The training went well, except for Lt. Robert Eybers, who suffered gear collapse. Fortunately the squadron's newly-formed crash crew/fire department was there to save the day.

The folks of the greater Sioux City area are quite used to claps of thunder, but sonic booms are another thing. Now that the 174th had the supersonic F-100, Lt. Col. Forney felt that the local citizenry should become familiar with this phenomenon, so Major Warren G. "Bud" Nelson took his F-100C to 20,000 feet, and at Mach 1.15 flew the 72 miles between Moville, Iowa, and Yankton, South Dakota, which included Sioux City in his flight path. Unfortunately, atmospheric conditions were such that the folks on the ground didn't get much of a rumble. The following Monday Major Nelson repeated his feat. To aid the citizens on the ground, Captain John J. Cottingham flew another F-100C at 40,000 feet just above Nelson. At this altitude vapor trails could be seen from the ground. It should be noted that the citizens of the Sioux City area had been notified of this exercise and why it was being carried out. In that notification, Lt. Col. Forney stated that no windows would be broken. Some of the glass in 100-year-old houses can be fragile, and apparently at least one window was broken as a result of this second try.

International tensions over East Germany, and Berlin in particular, heated up in June. U.S. President John F. Kennedy and Soviet Premier Nikita Khrushchev were practicing major brinksmanship. As the 174th was just entering the second third of their extended summer field training, they were notified that they were one of 64 Guard and seven Air Reserve outfits being notified of possible call-up because of the Berlin Crisis. These were the 64 units designated as priority groups if a national emergency should occur. Col. Forney stated that: "It's the type of alert for a small war. I'll let you know how I feel as soon as I pick myself up off the floor." It did mean that the training that they were then undergoing would be accelerated. Even though the crisis would draw out into November, the 174th was removed from the re-call list.

The end of an era also occurred in mid-August. On Sunday, August 13th, the last of the squadron's RF-84Fs were flown to Arizona to be put in mothball status. Out with the old and in with the new. On September 14th, one of the F-100s of the 174th opened the state plowing contest at Yankton, South Dakota, with a sonic boom.

March 1962 was a bad weather month; not unusual for the upper Midwest. Quite often, if one speaks of plowing ice or snow, a blade on the front of a truck or tractor is envisioned. The ice was so heavy in front of the 174th's hangar that the troops tied a farm plow onto an aircraft tug and literally plowed the heavy ice layer. A photo of this unusual action was picked up by the Associated Press and appeared in newspapers across the nation. More bad weather followed in late March, to the point that the Floyd River was approaching flood stage. Operation Hike Dike was put in place. At least half a million sandbags were needed along the 10-mile dike system. At 10 p.m. on Tuesday night, March 27th, the 174th Tactical Fighter Squadron was given a two-hour alert. Under the orders of Iowa governor Norman Erbe, the squadron was activated for two days. Some 200 members within a 50-mile radius of Sioux City, and more from as far as Omaha, Nebraska, reported in at midnight and joined Army National Guard and civilian volunteers. Roads, bridges, and farm land sustained severe damage. Families adjacent to dike areas had

Soviet Premier Nikita Khrushchev and U.S. President John F. Kennedy meet. The U.S. and Soviet Union would have a serious standoff. (*U.S. Department of State*)

The last, almost, of the squadron's RF-84Fs left Sioux City for Arizona August 13, 1961. A number would remain to be used for display. One of them is on the Sioux City ANG base today, along with other aircraft representing the unit's history. (*174th TFS/ McCallum collection*)

to be evacuated. Fortunately, damage within Sioux City was less due to all the volunteers that pitched in tirelessly.

Between May and October, runway work was being accomplished at Sioux City airport/Air Base and at Joe Foss Field, Sioux Falls, South Dakota. Some of the 174th aircraft and crews flew from Lincoln AFB, Nebraska, where the 173rd Fighter-Interceptor Squadron, which was expanded to the 155th Fighter-Interceptor Wing in 1960, flew their F-86L interceptors. At Sioux City, the 7,000-foot long runway was being lengthened to 8,900 feet. The shorter runways could be used by the Air Guard. As this was going on in Sioux City, Joe Foss Field was having runway work accomplished. The 114th Fighter Group of the South Dakota Air Guard had their Convair F-102 Delta Darts fly out of Sioux City for the summer.

In September 1962, a localized outbreak of diphtheria occurred in Sioux City. A supply of serum conjugate from Chicago was lost, and to get a replacement supply by scheduled airline would have taken an additional 24 hours; time was critical. The 174th Tactical Fighter Squadron was contacted, and an aircraft was sent to Chicago and returned with the much-needed resupply. Once again the 174th came through in an emergency.

Policy and attitude within the U.S. government, especially the USAF, slowly but surely aided the Air National Guard in becoming the force it is today. In July 1960, the USAF initiated the gaining command concept. In the past, the Continental

Air Command was responsible for the training of all reserve forces. Now the command which a reserve unit (Air National Guard or Air Force Reserve) would come under if called up, such as Tactical Air Command, would be responsible for that unit's training and operational performance. During the administration of President Dwight D. Eisenhower in the 1950s, nuclear deterrence and massive retaliation kept the Soviets in check to a certain point. During this period, strategic forces and associated weapon systems were the major thrust of the Department of Defense. In 1961, the administration of President John F. Kennedy announced a policy of flexible response; that is, wars engaged in would be managed and kept within acceptable non-nuclear limits. This brought about resurgence in tactical aviation. The Berlin Crisis, along with the units called up, once again showed the Air Guard's problems of lack of funding, low manning levels, and obsolete aircraft.

To strengthen the Air Guard, a number of squadrons were being brought to group strength. On October 1, 1962, the 185th Tactical Fighter Group received its federal recognition inspection and was formally constituted. Expanding to a higher echelon enabled the unit to be self-sufficient when called to active duty. Lt. Col. Donald W. Forney, who had been the 174th Tactical Fighter Squadron's commander, was appointed Group commander, with Lt. Col. Gale D. V. Stevens, formerly 174th Operations Officer, appointed Deputy Commander for Operations. Taking over the 174th as its commanding officer was Major Warren G. "Bud" Nelson, who had been Operations Supervisor and a flight leader. To staff the group, some personnel would be transferred from the 174th into either Group headquarters or one of the supporting squadrons. Some 380 additional personnel, both officers and enlisted, needed to be recruited. This brought the unit to over 800 personnel, nearly doubling its manpower. Unlike the 174th Tactical Fighter Squadron, the 185th Tactical Fighter Group had no lineage or honors linked to a World War II group, though the "185th" was linked to Sioux City. In the early 1940s, Headquarters Battery of the 2nd Battalion, 185th Field Artillery Regiment was stationed in Sioux City.

Mid-October 1962 had the newly-formed 185th Tactical Fighter Group wondering if they were going to be called up. Khrushchev and Kennedy were once again locking horns. What was to become the closest to nuclear war that the U.S. has ever seen became the Cuban Missile Crisis.

In many ways, the relationship between the active military forces and the reserves was somewhat love-hate. From the planning stages in the early 1940s to present, the active military establishment would try on a number of occasions to combine Guard and Reserve, or to eliminate them all together. The Guard and Reserve forces were a mixed bag, as far as their preparedness and capability went when called up for the Korea, Berlin, and Cuban emergencies. As the attempts failed to combine or eliminate the reserve forces, and as world conditions required their use, the active military would change from the attitude of doing away with them and make motions to rectify the neglect, underfunding, and lack of training and equipping that had been the norm for so long.

On October 1, 1962, the Sioux City unit became group strength. The new 185th Tactical Fighter Group was commanded by Lt. Col. Donald W. Forney. Taking over the slot of 174th Tactical Fighter Squadron commander was Major Warren G. Nelson, pictured above. (*174th TFS/McCallum collection*)

A c1963 view of the 185th TFG hangar and flight line showing one of its T-33s and a few F-100Cs. (*185th TFG/McCallum collection*)

On February 13, 1963, the Air Force published Air Force Regulation 45-60, "Programming, Equipping, and Maintaining the Capability of the Air Force Ready Reserve Forces." Mobilization Day (M-Day) had been the reserve forces' federal mission since 1945. This was a mission in which another World War II type of war would be fought. But the world situation had changed. What had been experienced, and was expected to be experienced, were not world-wide warfare, but localized conflicts, at the time called "brush fire wars," or low level counterinsurgencies. Under the M-Day scenario, and what had been experienced to a large extent in the three mobilizations since World War II, an extensive period of training and equipping was required after mobilization. Under AFR 45-60, the units were to be fully capable and equipped prior to mobilization.

The "gaining command" concept, along with AFR 45-60, would start to improve Air Force attitudes towards the Air Guard and give the Air Guard the ability to have a smoother integration with the active Air Force and the capability of performing the mission required. But to get to many parts of the world could be a problem. During the Berlin Crisis in 1961, 216 Air National Guard aircraft were sent to Europe to reinforce U.S. Air Forces in Europe (USAFE) under Operation Stair Step. Though capable pilots, the Air Guard pilots had to be trained for transoceanic flight, along with survival if a crash

1963 summer encampment at Volk Field, Wisconsin. Here one of the 174th TFS F-100s makes a strafing pass at the gunnery range. (*185th TFG/McCallum collection*)

A 174th F-100C in early squadron markings on a typical Iowa winter's day. (*185th TFS/McCallum collection*)

landing at sea would be experienced. Their aircraft were not equipped for inflight refueling, nor were the pilots trained in such operations. It took the Guard nearly a week to island-hop the Atlantic Ocean to their bases in Europe.

Air Refueling capability was needed for the Air Guard. Strategic Air Command was busy with the Southeast Asia war, along with their strategic duties, and could not fully support either Tactical Air Command (TAC) or USAFE with their KC-135 jet tankers. In 1960, the Air Guard was recommended to convert some squadrons to tankers. They were to get SAC's aging KC-97Gs as they were replaced by the KC-135. The first were received in July 1961. The Air Guard soon found that these lumbering giants, with four R-4360 reciprocating engines, lacked altitude and speed in performing the fighter refueling mission. Fortunately, the 126th Air Refueling Wing of the Illinois Air National Guard had an aeronautical engineer among their ranks. 1st Lt. Philip A. Meyer proposed hanging two J47 jet engines on the KC-97G in much the same manner as SAC had done with their KB-50s earlier. Thus, the KC-97L was born, and the Air Guard would not only be air refueling Guard planes, but those of TAC and USAFE.

In 1963, the Air Guard was ready to initiate long distance flights using air-to-air refueling. The 106th Tactical Reconnaissance Squadron of the Alabama Air National Guard had been called up during the Berlin crisis and had been part of Stair

In April 1963, the squadron's F-100s were sporting the new required markings. (*185th TFG/McCallum collection*)

Step. They were chosen to initiate the Guard's capability to perform this new task. In 1963, as a first step, they flew ten of their RF-84Fs to Puerto Rico in an exercise called Poncho. They were air-refueled by Air Guard KC-97s going and USAF KC-135s on their return trip. On August 30th, twelve of the squadron's RF-84Fs flew 3,500 miles to Alaska under exercise Minuteman Alpha. This was the longest duration Air Guard flight to date. Air Guard KC-97s provided the air refueling, while Air Guard C-97 transports provided airlift support. Not only did this effort prove Air Guard deployment capability, but while in Alaska, the 106th crews assisted Alaskan Air Command in photographing a considerable number of subject areas desired by the Command.

In November, other Air National Guard squadrons started performing such long range missions. On November 22nd, twelve F-100s of the District of Columbia's 121st Tactical Fighter Squadron, along with eight RF-84Fs of Missouri's 110th Tactical Fighter Squadron, assembled at Andrews AFB, Maryland, from which they flew to Ramey AFB, Puerto Rico, for exercise Cane Cutter. This was Air Guard's first non-stop, over water deployment. Seven days later, twelve F-100Cs of the 140th Tactical Fighter Wing of Denver, Colorado, and eight RF-84Fs of Mississippi's 152nd Tactical Reconnaissance Squadron, flew from Denver, Colorado, to Roosevelt Roads Naval Air Station, Puerto Rico, in exercise Abbey Tower.

In May 1963, the squadron was becoming proficient in aerial refueling. Here one of the 174th's F-100s is being "filled up" by an Illinois KC-97. (*185th TFG/McCallum collection*)

The Puerto Rico deployment team. From left to right are: Major Lawrence Kennedy, Major Lloyd A. Pippett, CMSgt Richard Dickson, SMSgt Lloyd Donovan, TSgt Marlin Noble, SSgt William Johnson, and Major Gordon L. Young. (*185th TFG/McCallum collection*)

December 1963 alert duty. (185th TFS/McCallum collection)

The 174th Tactical Fighter Squadron, under the 140th Tactical Fighter Wing, had been preparing for such missions. The squadron had been honing their aerial refueling skills since early 1963. In April, Major Warren Nelson, 174th commanding officer, took a ten-day trip to Italy. Arrangements were made for him to accompany an Air Force squadron based at Cannon AFB, New Mexico. Major Nelson rode with the squadron commander in a 2-place F-100F. The purpose of his trip was to experience a long range deployment in order to better understand the procedures and problems encountered. Squadron Operations Officer Major Gordon L. Young and Major Lawrence Kennedy, a flight leader, flew their F-100Cs to Denver to join up with the 140th Tactical Fighter Wing. Supporting the 174th were Major Lloyd A. Pippett, Chief of Maintenance, with four maintenance personnel (CM/Sgt Richard Dickson, SM/Sgt Lloyd Donovan, T/Sgt Marlin Noble, and S/Sgt William Johnson). The maintenance support personnel rendezvoused with other maintenance personnel in Denver and then flew to Puerto Rico by Air Guard C-97 transport. The purpose of Abbey Tower was not solely a deployment practice; while in Puerto Rico, they would undergo gunnery training. All had left Sioux City on November 29th, but the pilots arrived back on December 3rd, and the ground support personnel the following day. Flight time for the jets was 5 hours and 40 minutes. The ground personnel, flying by C-97, took about 14 hours to Denver, then flew back to Sioux City by C-47.

Joint Exercise Desert Strike was conducted by the U.S. Strike Command over two weeks in the latter part of May 1964. Involved were some 90,000 U.S. Army troops and 10,000 Air Force, including reserve forces. The 174th's aircraft were part of the 780 that participated in the exercise. The largest military war game since World War II, this exercise simulated a nuclear air and ground battle between two mythical forces. The area of the Mojave Desert included in this exercise was over 13 million acres of lands in the states of California, Nevada, and Arizona.

While the pilots and ground crew were stretching their wings over the ocean, the 185th Tactical Fighter Group made history back on base in the summer of 1963. Under revising manning allocations, which the Air Force was changing on a regular basis, the Group was allocated slots for three registered nurses. The first female in the 185th was Patricia Ann Stulich nee O'Brian. Miss O'Brian, an instructor in the operating room of St. Joseph Mercy hospital in Sioux City, and two friends saw an ad in a local newspaper and decided to inquire at the 185th. Only Miss O'Brien followed through and joined. She was commissioned a Second Lieutenant on September 15, 1963.

Air Guard to the rescue! On Friday, March 13, 1964, an Ozark Airlines Fairchild F-27 Friendship was approaching Sioux City Municipal Airport — which includes the air base and the 174th — for a landing when one of the passengers happened to look out and saw that one of the landing gear wheels was loose. One of the 174th's T-33 trainers was airborne on a training mission at the time the emergency was declared. The T-33 pilot flew in formation with the Ozark airliner and confirmed that the wheel was indeed loose. The airliner's pilot informed the tower that he was going to attempt a landing. The 185th Tactical Fighter Group was responsible for all runway and crash alerts between 8 o'clock in the morning and 4:30 in the afternoon. With the alert sounded, the 185th's ambulance, water tanker, fire crash rescue truck, and wrecker were dispatched and awaited what would happen. Fortunately, the wheel stayed on and the much-relieved passengers deplaned uninjured.

Firepower demonstration. In July 1964, the Army National Guard's 34 (Red Bull) Division, which had units from a number of midwestern states, including Iowa, was to hold its two-week summer encampment at Camp Ripley, Minnesota. There was a large parade of over 6,000 Iowa troops. Present were National Guard, state, city, and civic leaders in the reviewing stands. Besides the dignitaries there were friends and families of the troops. Included was a firepower demonstration by the 174th Tactical Fighter Squadron firing anti-armor missiles from their F-100Cs.

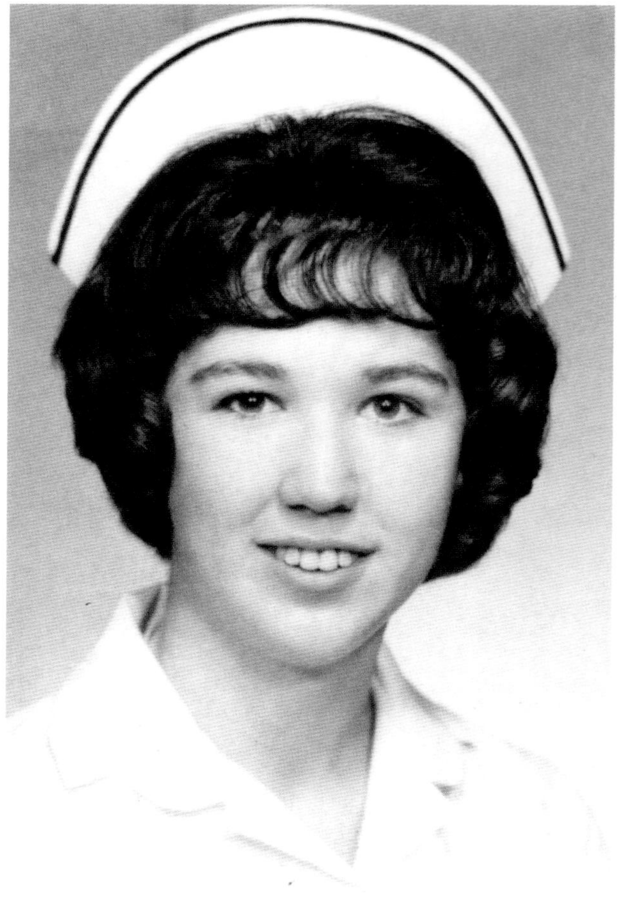

In 1963, the 185th Tactical Fighter Group acquire its first female member, Patricia Ann O'Brian. (*185th TFG/McCallum collection*)

In August 1964, Sioux City held their fourth annual Air Exposition at the Municipal Airport. Included in the Exposition were static displays of military and commercial aircraft, along with flight demonstrations by the Navy's Blue Angels and North American Aviation test pilot turned exhibition pilot Bob Hoover flying his yellow P-51 Mustang. On Sunday afternoon, August 9th, there

A formation of 174th F-100s glide through the skies of the upper Midwest. (*185th TFG/McCallum collection*)

A "Dart" target is affixed to a squadron F-100. Hopefully the other pilots who will be firing at the Dart will not accidently hit the tow aircraft. (*185th TFG/McCallum collection*)

Armorers arm a 174th F-100 for gunnery practice. (*185th TFG/McCallum collection*)

The big race of 1964: Captain Eddie Ricketyback (Shelby Hagberg) in his Waco biplane versus Capt. Dick Strohmeier in his F-100C. (*185th TFG/McCallum collection*

was what the *Sioux City Journal* called the "Race of the Century." The competition was between one of the 174th Tactical Fighter Squadron's F-100Cs and a Waco biplane. The Waco belonged to Shelby Hagberg, a well-known Midwest pilot and curator of the Mid-Continent Air Museum at the airport, who supposedly instigated the whole affair. Flying against Mr. Hagberg in his Waco was Captain Dick Strohmeier for the 174th.

To make the race a balanced affair, the Waco was to circle Sioux City while the F-100 was to fly to Omaha, Nebraska, and back. Hagberg took off in Old Rickitiback (his Waco) and started putting around Sioux City. To keep the 60,000 spectators informed of the Waco's progress, local radio station KMNS had its radio car follow the plane up Interstate 29 while feeding its progress via radio back to the airport. Due to air traffic in the Omaha area, the route of the F-100 was changed to Sioux Falls, South Dakota, at the last minute. Sioux Falls is about the same air miles from Sioux City as is Omaha.

Stories of the race linger today. It is rumored that Col. Forney strongly suggested, some say ordered, that Captain Strohmeier win. Apparently, as Strohmeier was approaching the north end of Sioux City on his return flight he heard that the Waco was approaching the airport, so he picked up the pace. He kicked in the afterburner, though trying to keep the speed at Mach .90 in order to stay out of the transition zone. Apparently he failed.

He was still in afterburner when he crossed the airfield. He thought he had pulled it off and landed. As Col. Forney approached the F-100, Strohmeier wondered if he was going to get an "Atta boy." Some of Forney's first words went something like "I got ten @$*!#&%# phone calls about what you did!" Windows were apparently broken in a number of homes and businesses, including a hospital. He was later told that he had shock waves showing when he crossed the airfield. That was not the end of it. Col. Forney had to make a couple of trips to Washington, D.C., to do some fast explaining. Captain Strohmeier wondered if he would lose his

The 174th team supporting Operation Ready Go. After nine hours flying across the Atlantic, the 174th pilots landed at Hahn AB, Germany, where within four hours they were mission ready. (*185th TFG/McCallum collection*)

to Washington, D.C., to do some fast explaining. Captain Strohmeier wondered if he would lose his wings. Apparently Forney told a good story, and Strohmeier kept on flying.

During the Berlin Crisis, the Air Guard deployed aircraft to Europe to reinforce USAFE. Without the capability for air refueling, it took the Air Guard about a week to reach their destination. Operation Ready Go, in August 1964, was meant to show what a trained and capable Air Guard could do. Utilizing air refueling, 19 F-100s, including 174th Tactical Fighter Squadron aircraft, and 12 RF-84Fs flew non-stop to Europe in nine hours. Flying for the 174th were Capt. Jerry Edwards, Lt. Gordon Goodier, Lt. Ron Lenagh, and Lt. Ron G. Heitritter. They landed at Hahn AB, Germany. Four hours after arrival they

Operation Ready Go pilots from the 174th preparing for the mission outside of the squadron ready room. (*185th TFG/McCallum collection.*

The Ready Go pilots for the 174th were: Lt. Gordon W. Goodier, Lt. Ronald G. Heitritter, Lt. Ronald F. Lenagh, and Capt. Jerry Edwards. (*185th TFG/McCallum collection*)

The F-100 was much more than a tactical nuclear bomber. It was also an excellent ground support and interdiction aircraft. The pilots were learning to be proficient in dive bombing, skip bombing, high and low angle strafing, and air-to-air gunnery. Over the bombing and gunnery ranges the crews dropped bombs, fired missiles, and fired their 20 millimeter cannons. At summer training in June 1964, the scores were quite impressive, but in August, every pilot fired an AIM-9 Sidewinder missile and hit the target 26 out of 26 times.

Alaskan Air Command conducted back-to-back joint Army/Air Force exercises. Exercise Diamond Lil XIV was between September and October 4, 1964, with Denali Eagle following from October 5th through the 10th. Operating as a separate unit out of Elmendorf AFB, the 14th Tactical Fighter Wing (out of Denver, Colorado) augmented active duty forces engaged in this arctic training operation. The Wing was supported by the 140th Tactical Fighter Group (Denver), 184th Tactical Fighter Group (Wichita, Kansas), 185th Tactical Fighter Group/174th Tactical Fighter Squadron (Sioux City, Iowa), and 150th Tactical Fighter Group (Albuquerque, New Mexico). The 185th/174th was headed by Lt. Col. Donald W. Forney, with the participation of 17 of the squadron pilots supported by 47 enlisted personnel. Air Guard and USAF tanker and transport aircraft supported the fighter deployment.

The exercise consisted of two Army brigades maneuvering in Alaska's vast back country. The Air Guard fighters flew close ground support for friendly

Operation Diamond Lil was a real exercise, but this photo was a tongue-in-cheek announcement of that operation. Here group commander Lt. Col. Forney and Sergeants Dale L. McCuddin and Donald M. Risdal pose with survival equipment. (*185th TFG/ McCallum collection*)

One of the 174th's F-100s operating out of Elmendorf AFB, Alaska, during operation Diamond Lil. (*185th TFG/McCallum collection*)

forces and flew interdiction missions against the opposing forces. They also got great experience in working with forward air controllers (FACs), who would identify potential targets for the F-100s to hit. At the conclusion of the exercises, General Walter C. Sweeney, Jr., Tactical Air Command, stated that, "The execution of this deployment in such an exemplary manner conclusively demonstrated the professional competence of the participating aircrews as well as supervisory and support personnel."

Someone on the 185th Tactical Fighter Group's newsletter, the *Group Post*, apparently had a sense of humor. In the January 1965 issue of *Group Post*, "an urgent call went out" for Father Marvin Boes "to report to the Orderly Room to fill out AF Form 869 Religious Preference Card."

The first half of 1965 was not a good time for Sioux City F-100s and one of its pilots. On February 5th, two of the jets were flying a routine training mission. Lt. Col. Ellis L. Fisher, an Air Force officer and adviser to the 185th Tactical Fighter Group, was flying one. He was accompanied by Lt. Douglas J. Feauto, a pilot with the 174th Tactical Fighter Squadron. As they were landing, the brakes on one of the planes' landing gear failed and that plane veered into the other. Neither pilot was injured. In May, Lt. Feauto was once again landing at Sioux City Municipal Airport when his F-100 was hit by wind and it went off the runway, collapsing the nose gear. Fortunately, Lt. Feauto was not injured this time, either.

In mid-year, a military buildup was taking place in Southeast Asia. Though President Lyndon B. Johnson refused to mobilize the reserve forces, some of them would be prepared for such action. In August, Secretary of Defense McNamara's Selected Reserve Force program was announced. Under this program, selected units were authorized to recruit to 100 percent manning and receive

This June 1966 photo shows the beginning of the changeover from natural metal to camouflage for the 174th's F-100s. (*185th TFG/McCallum collection*)

stepped up training. The purpose was to make the units ready to deploy on 24 hours notice by the end of August 1966. The Air Force authorized 38 Air Force Reserve and Air Guard units for this program. Nine Air National Guard fighter groups (all F-100 units), four tactical reconnaissance groups, and one tactical control group were chosen. Within the Air Force the program was initially called "Beef Broth," and later "Combat Beef."

The National Guard Bureau notified each unit on August 10th. The 185th Tactical Fighter Group was one of the nine tactical fighter groups under Beef Broth. Immediately they made plans to increase their personnel by 140 to bring it up to a full strength of 793, both officers and enlisted. By the end of August, all 140 additional personnel had been recruited, with some coming from a waiting list the Group had established some time back. They reached full manning by year's end. Besides the increased manning and intensified training, equipment was also being modernized and brought up to full requirements.

As part of the strengthening of the Air Guard, all F-100 fighter units under Tactical Air Command underwent organizational changes. These changes were in the support area, where Consolidated Aircraft Maintenance Squadrons were created. Within the 185th Tactical Fighter Group, Major Lloyd A. Pippett, Chief of Maintenance, got the additional responsibility of Consolidated Aircraft Maintenance Squadron commander effective December 14, 1965.

Whether marching, or in aircraft maintenance training, or weapons loading class, the 185th Tactical Fighter Group was on accelerated training full force as 1966 opened. Thirty pilots, including Group commander Col. Forney and 174th commander Lt. Col. Nelson, flew to Cannon AFB, New Mexico, in late January to qualify in air-to-air weaponry.

Classroom work was carried out at Cannon AFB, after which the pilots flew their F-100Cs to the gunnery range at Holloman AFB, New Mexico. Over the range an aircraft towed a "dart" target on a 1,500-foot cable. The "dart" measured 16 feet long by five feet wide at the base. To qualify, the pilots had to make two sorties. At the end of the training the pilots had flown about 42 sorties.

The entire 185th Tactical Fighter Group had to show themselves ready and capable for mobilization. Their summer field training at Volk Field, Wisconsin, was more than two weeks practicing their profession. Under the watchful eye of a Tactical Air Command inspection team, the 185th underwent their annual Operational Readiness Inspection at Volk Field. The inspection team consisted of Field Grade officers, including an "informal" visit by TAC commander General Gabriel P. Disosway.

The Operational Readiness Inspection had been initiated in June at the 185th's base in Sioux City, Iowa, but the aerial gunnery had to be completed while at summer field training. From Volk Field, the pilots flew 54 sorties over the gunnery range at Lake Michigan, where they performed air-to-air gunnery. They also flew 60 air-to-ground sorties in strafing and bombing, and rockets were fired. The pilots had to qualify biannually with the AIM-9B Sidewinder air intercept missile.

In late March/early April 1967, Air Proving Ground Center, Eglin AFB, Florida (part of Air Force Systems Command), initiated an eight-day test program in Alaska to conduct napalm bomb tests under cold conditions (near 30 degrees below zero). 185th Tactical Fighter Group pilots and support personnel carried out the tests. Lt. Col. Gordon L. Young, Captain Jerry Edwards, and 1st Lt. Jon P. Haddock flew their F-100Cs to Eielson AFB, Fairbanks, Alaska, non-stop with the aid of a SAC KC-135 tanker. A full support team, with tons of equipment and supplies, was airlifted to Eielson AFB by Air Force C-130. The support team included 18 airmen led by Major Lloyd A. Pippett, Consolidated Aircraft Maintenance Squadron commander, and Major James A. Konopisos, deputy commander of materiel. The tests were carried out over the bombing and gunnery range near Fort Greely. About 18 sorties were flown, dropping about 36 napalm bombs.

The 185th Tactical Fighter Group almost lost its commanding officer, as well as Iowa's Adjutant General, in August. On August 9th, Col. Donald W. Forney was to fly Iowa Adjutant General Junior F. Miller from Sioux City to Washington, D.C., for a meeting at the Pentagon. Flying in a two-place

Colonel Forney solos a soapbox. (*185th TFG/McCallum collection*)

F-100F borrowed from the Missouri Air National Guard, the two took off from Sioux City Municipal Airport. Some 15 minutes out Col. Forney incurred a flameout. He tried to restart the engine two or three times with no success. As he was attempting the restart, he started to circle back to the airport. They found that they were not going to make it back, so they ejected over farmland near Dennison, Iowa. Forney was uninjured, but Miller had bruises on his legs from the ejection. He was kept in a local hospital overnight. Apparently things could have been much worse for the Adjutant General, as he had some problems with his parachute chords in the beginning and was quite close to power lines when coming in for his landing. The two airmen were greeted by a number of farmers awaiting them, followed soon by a highway patrol car which took them to the hospital.

In the summer of 1967, there was much unrest in the country over the war in southeast Asia. Riots were breaking out, including one in nearby Milwaukee, Wisconsin, in late July. The National Guard, Air as well as Army, were being called out to quell the disturbances. Though riot control was considered a major function of the Air Police in the 1960s, about 400 troops of the 185th underwent riot training during their weekend stint of September 9th and 10th. The instructors were provided by Sioux City's 2nd Mechanized Battalion, 33rd Infantry Regiment, Army National Guard.

Surprise! On November 17th, 832nd Air Division director of operations Col. Jackson Saunders (Cannon AFB, New Mexico), 140th Tactical Fighter Wing commander Brig. Gen. Walter E. Williams (Denver, Colorado), TAC inspector general Brig. Gen. Dewitt R. Searles (Langley AFB, Virginia), and chief of the inspection division at TAC, Col. John S. Clarke, arrived at the 185th for a No Notice Operational Readiness Inspection. Once again, the 185th proved itself manned, capable, and ready. But was something in the wind?

Chapter Eight

The Bats of Vietnam

It was high noon in Korea (January 23, 1968), but 10 o'clock at night (January 22nd) in Washington, D.C., when the U.S. Navy's intelligence ship, the USS *Pueblo* (AGER-2), collecting signals intelligence off the North Korean coast, was approached by a North Korean subchaser. According to the *Pueblo*, they were about 17 nautical miles off the North Korean coast and 24 nautical miles from Wonsan. Soon the subchaser was joined by three patrol boats and MiG-15 jet fighters. Within two and a half hours the incident was over, and the ship and its crew were under North Korean control.

First reaction came when Pacific Air Forces was directed to deploy 12 F-105s and eight F-4Cs to Osan AB, South Korea. The next movement was for the aircraft carrier *Enterprise* and Task Group 70.6 to move to approximately 40 nautical miles off of Pusan, with an estimated time of arrival of 6:00 p.m. on the 24th, Eastern Standard Time. President Lyndon B. Johnson considered using air power to free the ship and crews, but his air commanders had all they could do with the war in Vietnam and elsewhere. All resources were stretched to the maximum. On January 26th, the Central Intelligence Agency had one of its A-12 reconnaissance aircraft make a three-pass mission over the southern part of North Korea and the Demilitarized Zone. The North Koreans were not preparing for military action.

The South Koreans were not convinced. They were quite concerned that the North was up to no good. They wanted some show of force by the U.S., or they would pull their troops out of

The U.S. Navy's intelligence ship *USS Pueblo* (AGER-2) was captured by the North Koreans some 24 nautical miles off of Wonsan on January 23, 1968. There was some speculation that the North Koreans might be contemplating invading their neighbors to the south. (*U.S. Navy*)

This North Korean chart shows where they claimed to have captured the *USS Pueblo*. (*U.S. Navy*)

One of the first changes to the 174th Tactical Fighter Squadron's F-100Cs upon mobilization was removal of Air National Guard and State markings. (*185th TFS/McCallum collection*)

Vietnam. On January 25th, President Johnson issued Executive Order 11392, which mobilized 9,341 Air Guardsmen, plus reservists from the other services. Amongst the wings and groups mobilized were the 140th Tactical Fighter Wing and its three groups, including the 185th Tactical Fighter Group. The 140th was informed that there was possible deployment overseas within 72 hours.

Shortly before noon on Thursday, January 25th, the 185th Tactical Fighter Group received official word that they were being mobilized. They were given 36 hours to muster their troops. As one of the groups under the Beef Broth/Combat Beef program, they were combat ready and capable of mustering within 24 hours. At 7:00 in the morning on Saturday, January 27th, all 860 members of the 185th were ready. Not present was one man home sick with the mumps and another traveling in Europe whom they had not been able to contact. Quite impressive was the fact that a good number of their pilots were airline pilots, and were scattered around the country. Because of their airline jobs, some of these pilots lived in such places as Dallas, Fort Lauderdale, New York, Seattle, Denver, Chicago, and Minneapolis.

From expecting to be shipped out within hours to wondering for three months what was going to happen was the plight of the Air Guard units called up in January. The *Pueblo* incident was not leading to an escalation of force. Policy makers in Washington, D.C., were debating what to do with the Air Guard mobilized at their home bases. The Air Force really only wanted the flying squadrons, and they could have been called solely, but were not. The North Vietnamese and their Viet Cong allies conducted the Tet Offensive between January 30th and February 25th. Though the enemy offensive was beaten off, the American citizenry back home was turning against the war.

The usual processing, clothing and equipment checks, and general getting ready were going on in the 185th. In preparation for going overseas, practice shooting was taking place at the firing range. The pilots were doing some "polishing" on their skills, as Col. Forney put it. The Sioux City Air Base did not have accommodations for the entire Wing. Those that lived within driving distance to the base could go home when off duty. Those that lived further away were put up at the Sheraton-Warrior hotel in Sioux City. In mid-February, a briefing was given to the wives of Air Guardsmen mobilized to explain their privileges and responsibilities. Some 460 wives met at the Base theater, where they heard from Col. Forney, the Base executive officer, and others on legal rights, medical services, and personal services, as well as talks by the chaplain and Red Cross representative.

Explanation for the wives of the 185th Tactical Fighter Group personnel what could be expected with the mobilization and what services would be available to them during this period of mobilization. (*185th TFG/McCallum collection*)

During the second half of February, the 140th Wing and its four groups were getting the idea that they were not going to Korea, but to Vietnam. The Wing and its pilots from the four Groups would be going to Cannon AFB, New Mexico, for seven weeks of training in two courses called Night Owl and Top Off. On March 4th, 30 airmen—about half were maintenance specialists—left Sioux City by Air Force C-118 transport. Two C-130s hauled equipment for the group. Six pilots led by Major Dudley P. Smidt followed in their F-100Cs. Over the seven weeks of the course, pilots and support personnel would be rotating between Sioux City and Cannon AFB to give the experience to as many as possible.

The fighter pilots would find the experience much like they would experience in Vietnam, as they would be working with Forward Air Controllers (FACs). The training consisted of night delivery of weapons and delivery of heavy loads of weapons. They flew over a special range in the desert where they attacked mock-Viet Cong and North Vietnamese installations. They were quite

To prepare the 174th's pilots for their mission, they were sent to Cannon AFB, New Mexico, where they participated in Night Owl and Top Off. Here they are dropping ordnance on the bombing range. (*185th TFS/McCallum collection*)

realistic, as they included tunnel systems and air-to-air missile sites.

During late March and early April, a number of the pilots attended Tactical Air Command's Life Support School at Homestead AFB, Florida. Those pilots that had attended the course the previous year did not have to attend. This sea survival course consisted of class instruction, which included the handling of life support gear from radios to life rafts. Each phase of class instruction included a dunk in Biscayne Bay at the end of the day, where the pilots demonstrated what they had learned. The concluding test was greater than any thrill ride at your favorite amusement park. Each pilot was strapped into a special parachute designed as a parasail and pulled off the deck of a modified landing craft by a speed boat. When airborne, the trainee could go as high as the tow rope would allow. The rope was cut loose, and the pilot descended into Biscayne Bay, where he employed the lessons learned up to then.

Dissatisfaction over how the Air National Guard units were called up for the *Pueblo* crisis was expressed during the months that the units waited for something to happen. Much is still being written about the helter skelter way the units were broken up and scattered all over. A lot of money, time, and effort under Beef Broth was spent to make the units combat ready and able within hours after mobilization to go to any unimproved base and set up operations immediately as a self-sustained unit. But this call up did just the opposite.

An excellent example of this was the 140th Tactical Fighter Wing, stationed at Buckley ANG Base near Denver, Colorado. At the time of the mobilization, the 140th Tactical Fighter Wing was composed of the following groups and flying squadrons: 140th Tactical Fighter Group/120th Tactical Fighter Squadron at Buckley ANG Base, near Denver, Colorado; 184th Tactical Fighter Group/127th Tactical Fighter Squadron at McConnell AFB, near Wichita, Kansas; 185th Tactical Fighter Group/174th Tactical Fighter Squadron near Sioux City, Iowa; and the 150th Tactical Fighter Group/188th Tactical Fighter Squadron at Kirtland AFB, near Albuquerque, New Mexico.

Unlike what they trained for and expected, only the flying squadrons of the 140th Tactical Fighter Wing and varying quantities of support personnel from their groups were dispatched overseas. The 120th, 174th, and 188th Tactical Fighter Squadrons were sent to three bases in South Vietnam (aka the Republic of Vietnam), while the 127th went to South Korea. A fourth Air Guard squadron was sent to South Vietnam, but it was the 136th Tactical Fighter Squadron from New York. The 140th Tactical Fighter Wing headquarters was reduced to 16 officers and 20 enlisted airmen within a couple of weeks after the 120th Tactical Fighter Squadron's departure for Vietnam, and was relocated to Cannon AFB, near Clovis, New Mexico. The wings commander, Brig. Gen. Walter E. Williams, was reassigned to Vietnam in early June. Here they would perform Forward Air Controller and Combat Crew Training.

Decisions were made in late April about which units were going to Vietnam. First to depart was

For those who needed water survival training, or who would have to renew their training while overseas, they attended the course at Homestead AFB, Florida. (*185th TFS/McCallum collection*)

These are the pilots of the 185th TFG, including the 174th TFS. In the front row are, from left to right: Gordon Young (174th TFS commander), Darrell Lake, Edward Hearter, Kulday Visnapuu, John McClellan, Jr., Robert Eybers, Warren Brown (the only 174th pilot killed in Vietnam), Dudley Smidt, Jon Haddock, and Donald Lundvall. In the middle row are: John Haley, Patrick Parks, Clive Grewell, David Wilson, William Bowen, Robert Anderson, Lyle Bainbridge, Charles Blumer, Shirley Watson, Donald Forney (185th TFG commander), and Norman Schaap. In the back row are: John Miller, Gordon Goodier, Sherman Sawin, Eugene Atkinson, Charles Bradley, Ronald Heitritter, Michael McLean, Benton Boyer, Jerry Edwards, Robert Ray, Ronald Lenagh, and Bruce Mosier. (*185th ARW*)

the 120th, which left on the 28th and arrived at Phan Rang AB, Republic of Vietnam, May 3rd. The 174th was next to leave. Because of a shortage of support personnel at the base they were going to, a large percentage of the 185th Consolidated Aircraft Maintenance Squadron would accompany the 174th. With only two or so weeks' notice, they were busy with last minute preparations. At one point Col. Donald Forney, 185th Tactical Fighter Group commander, called Lt. Col. Lloyd A. Pippett, Consolidated Aircraft Maintenance Squadron, into his office and asked how many of the fleet of 25 F-100Cs were available to make the long flight to Southeast Asia? There were 22. Air Force orders limited the number of pilots that the 174th could

Lt. Col. Lloyd A. Pippett, 185th Consolidated Maintenance Squadron commander. (*185th TFG/McCallum collection*)

One of the many C-141 Starlifters to arrive at Sioux City to carry equipment, spare parts, and personnel to Vietnam. The C-141s were based out of Travis AFB, California, and McChord AFB, Washington. (*185th TFG/McCallum collection*)

take, so the hard decision of who would go had to be made. Besides the 22 flying the F-100s, three back-up pilots would travel by C-141 transport.

From Travis AFB in California and McChord AFB in Washington state, the large Military Airlift Command Lockheed C-141 Starlifters started arriving on Saturday, May 11th, with a total of 10 of the large cargo aircraft arriving and leaving that weekend. Spare and repair parts, including engines, test equipment, tools, and all kinds of general supplies, were loaded aboard. Only a few of the 185th personnel accompanied these loads.

On Tuesday, May 14th, friends, families, and loved ones were at Sioux City Air Base to see the troops off. Loading into three additional C-141 transports was most of the 185th Consolidated Aircraft Maintenance Squadron and about 50 other support personnel—clerks, cooks, air police, barber, and the like. Starting at 8:06 a.m., Lt. Col. Gordon L. Young, 174th commander, led a flight of six F-100s into the air. Each flight headed north to make a pass over Sioux City before heading for Southeast Asia. Following him at 30-minute intervals were two more flights of six and a final flight of four. The three C-141s, with the last of the equipment and over 300 men, took off following the fighters. Col. Forney was not there to see his troops off. He had gone to Ellsworth AFB, near Rapid City, South Dakota. There he joined Brig. Gen. Walter E. Williams, 140th Tactical Fighter Wing commander, in an Air Force C-135 airborne command plane to oversee the deployment. Forney arrived back in Sioux City via commercial airliner that Sunday, the 19th.

The call-up of the 185th Tactical Fighter Group proved to be an immense fiscal impact to the greater Sioux City area, especially as the airmen were shipped out to parts all over the world. The impact, in 1968 dollars, was around $2 million dollars in

Waves of 174th F-100s departed Sioux City, Iowa, for a destination then unknown. On their long journey they would use aerial refueling from KC-135 tankers and island stops along the way. (*185th TFG/ McCallum collection*)

Fellow guardsmen, family, friends, and the community saw the pilots in their F-100s off to war, as well as all the other troops by air transport. (*185th TFG/McCallum collection*)

payroll and a loss in expenditures of over $225 million. It even got worse, as Army National Guard units were mobilized, especially for the town of Le Mars, which is about 25 miles from Sioux City. There was also the financial impact on the airmen and their families. A good example was the bank vice president, who found himself and his family suddenly living on the pay of an Airman Second Class. Quite a difference.

The 174th Tactical Fighter Squadron arrived at Phu Cat AB on Friday, May 17th. Phu Cat was one of the newest and safest bases. Phu Cat had opened for operations in early 1967. Part of its safety was attributed to the 5,000 Republic of Korea (South Korea) troops that were guarding part of the base. They were well known for their ferocity, which probably attributed to a story that a number of the 174th personnel brought back. The story goes that when the Koreans caught a number of the enemy they took two of them up in a helicopter. Then they would throw one of them out of the helicopter without a parachute. They would then question the remaining prisoner. Apparently these actions usually loosened the tongue of the remaining prisoner. Located in a remote area in Binh Dinh province, it was 275 miles northeast of Saigon and 19 miles northwest of Qui Nhon, a coastal port on the South China Sea. At Phu Cat, the 174th became part of the 37th Tactical Fighter Wing. Welcoming the 174th was Col. LeRoy J. Manor, the Wing's commander. Col. Manor was in his position as commander only for two days at that time. They were also greeted by General William W. Momyer, who commanded the 7th Air Force.

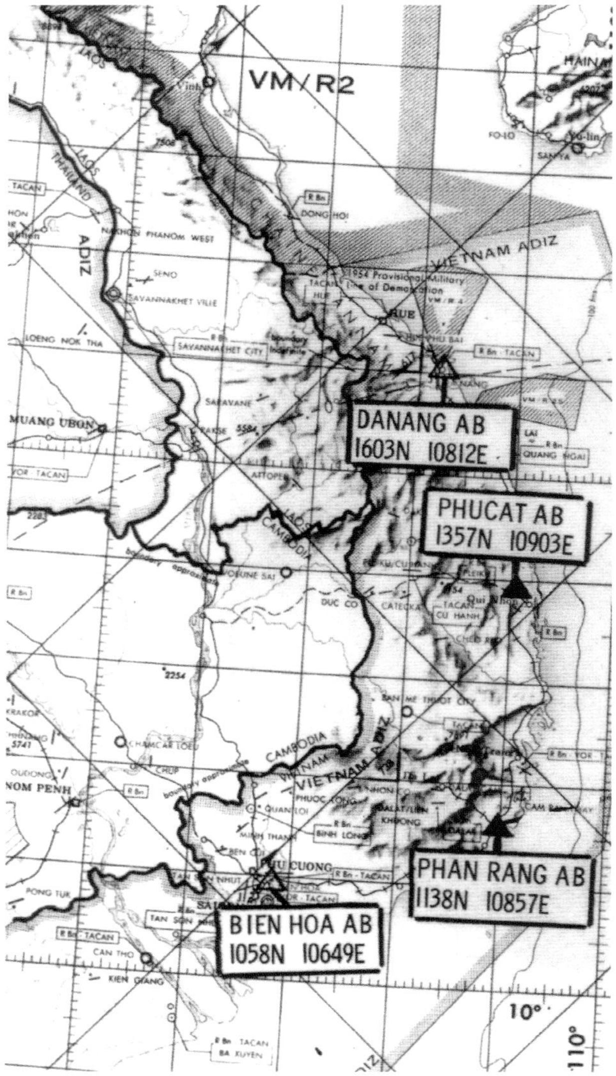

Vietnam. (*USAF*)

As the 174th Tactical Fighter Squadron and 185th Consolidated Aircraft Maintenance Squadron personnel settled in, they were assigned organizational responsibilities. Lt. Col. Gordon L. Young commanded the 174th, which included 29 officers and 129 airmen. The 185th CAMS was integrated within 37th Tactical Fighter Wing organizations. The 185th troops ended up taking responsible positions heading maintenance shops. Lt. Col. Lloyd A. Pippett became the 37th's maintenance control officer.

An interesting outcome of the Vietnam experience would be that the squadrons would become known by their radio call signs. The call sign for the 174th was Bat. As they became known as "The Bats" in Vietnam, they have continued to be known by that moniker yet today. They have even used a bat cartoon on the tails of their aircraft since that time.

Also at Phu Cat, under the 37th, was the 416th Tactical Fighter Squadron. They became well known for flying two-place F-100Fs in what was originally called the Commando Sabre Operation. Their radio call sign was Misty, which they are still well known as today. Their mission as Fast Forward Air Controllers, or Fast FACs, was to fly fast and low over enemy territory, acting as the eyes for the

The landscape of Phu Cat. (*185th TFG/McCallum collection*)

174th TFS had a supurb operational ready rate; the experience and expertise of its maintenance personnel and the pilots impressed all with their accuracy and determination to hit the target. (*National Guard Bureau/History Office*)

Phu Cat AB, Vietnam. This is what the F-100 pilots and the C-141s carrying all of the 174th's baggage saw as they were coming in. (*185th TFG/McCallum collection*)

ground attack fighters armed with bombs and rockets. Misty's first commanding officer was Col. George E. "Bud" Day, of Sioux City, Iowa. The dangerous mission of the Mistys saw 34 of them shot down (22 percent). Col. Day was one of these; he, too, was shot down the August prior to the 174th's arrival. Col. Day was captured and remained a prisoner 67 months. He was awarded the Medal of Honor.

Besides the 416th and its F-100Fs, the 355th Tactical Fighter Squadron and Detachment 1, 612th Tactical Fighter Squadron, operated out of Phu Cat and were assigned to the 37th Tactical Fighter Wing. These squadrons flew the F-100D. The missions for the 37th Tactical Fighter Wing and its F-100Cs and Ds were to fly interdiction, bombardment, escort, and close air support. In the close and direct air support roles, they operated closely with FACs flying in light, single-engine aircraft in support of American, Vietnamese, and other allied military.

If the "regulars" in Vietnam wondered how a bunch of farmers and small town folks were going to perform in combat, they soon found out. At the time the 174th arrived in Vietnam, it was taking Air Force pilots an average 20 orientation flights to be operationally ready. It took the 174th five! Within 11 days after arrival, all of the squadron's pilots were operationally ready. That meant that they had concluded theater indoctrination, tropical survival at Clark AFB in the Philippines, and three missions. Major Eugene T. Atkinson, known as "The Judge," flew the squadron's first mission May 20th. In that mission hits were made on a missile site and a bunker complex. The first missions were in North Vietnam, above the Demilitarized Zone.

A typical mission was one flown on June 24, 1968. On this mission Capt. Darrell F. Lake, call sign Bat 41, was flying lead. 1st Lt. Charles J. Blumer, Bat 42, was on Lake's wing, while Maj. Robert C. Eybers, Bat 43, was element lead. Element lead would take over if lead lost radio contact, or was damaged to an extent he could no longer perform his duties.

As usual, Frag Orders came down from Tactical Air Control Center that morning. A Frag meant Fragmentary; an abbreviated form of an operation order, usually issued on a day-to-day basis. Included in these orders were the targets to be hit that day. At a pre-mission briefing the crews got target, weather, and other intelligence information, including status of friendly forces in the area. From there they would go to their aircraft and perform preflight checks.

Major Eugene T. Atkinson. (*185th TFG/McCallum collection*)

Capt. Darrell E. Lake. (*185th TFG/McCallum collection*)

The three 174th F-100s went out to the active runway and contacted the local control, call sign Sun Valley. They requested clearance from Sun Valley,

Major Robert C. Eybers (*185th TFG/McCallum collection*)

1st Lt. Charles J. Blumer. (*185th TFG/McCallum collection*)

Ordnance loaded, and this F-100 of the 174th is just about ready to go. This is a typical revetment at Phu Cat AB. (*185th TFG/ McCallum collection*)

performed radio and IFF check, requested status of artillery fire within the area of Phu Cat, then taxied and took off. After getting airborne, they contacted traffic control, call sign Panama. They requested and received permission to contact Helix Control, the FAC frequency for the area they would be working in, in this case Chu Lai. From Helix Control they received permission to contact the FAC that they would be working with. In this instance it was Helix 11 (Helix One One).

They had to wait a while, as Helix 11 was currently working with other F-100s. When finished, he contacted Bat 41 and requested their status. Capt. Lake informed him that they were a flight of four Fox One Hundreds, mission 6014. The FAC asked what weapons they had onboard (six rockets and six Mark 117 low drags [a 750-pound bomb]). If there were degrees of danger, the FAC had to be at the top of the list, and their losses show it (which is one of the reasons that the Fast FAC program was started). Flying in a light, single-engine airplane, Helix 11 had located a bunker system. His instruction to Capt. Lake and his flight of F-100s was that the river, which Lake confirmed he saw, came to a big Y. There was a big horseshoe, with the closed end points towards the ocean. Friendlies were four and a half kilometers east of the river, and the target was

Lt. Col. Gordon L. Young marks one of the places that his Supersabre was hit by ground fire. Colonel Young was fortunate, in that he was able to set his damaged craft down at Da Nang AB, north of Phu Cat. (*185th TFG/McCallum collection*)

on the west side. It was a triangle trench bunker type complex, with two automatic weapons positioned in the center on top of the hill. The FAC wasn't sure if the weapons were manned.

To assist, the FAC fired smoke rockets at the target to aid in identification. The F-100s made multiple strikes on the target, with the FAC assisting in providing preferred direction of attack as seen from his vantage point. When they had unloaded their stores on the target the FAC commented: "About two weeks ago I could have used bombing like this." The FAC made his bomb damage assessment and gave them a 95 over 100. They had three direct hits and three within 50 feet. They did not get 100/100 because one of the direct hits was a dud.

By the first week of July, the 174th was performing stunningly. They were flying in areas around the Demilitarized Zone, the Ho Chi Minh Trail, and the northern regions of the country, where they drew more enemy fire than other areas. At this time, the 174th had completed its 1,000th combat mission. Though their aircraft received damage from ground fire, it would become deadly in July. On the 8th, Lt. Col. Gordon L. Young was on a mission against an antiaircraft position in the northern regions of South Vietnam when his F-100 was heavily damaged by ground fire. He completed his attack and was able to land his crippled fighter at Da Nang AB. The colonel was unhurt, but his plane needed to be repaired before it could return to Phu Cat.

But on the 14th, 1st Lt. Warren K. Brown was not as fortunate. While on a mission 24 miles southwest of Hue, near the A Shau Valley, Lt. Brown's F-100 was hit by ground fire on his second pass at the target. He radioed to his wingmen that his aircraft had been struck by ground fire and started a pull-up. His two flight members tried to keep him in sight, but lost Lt. Brown in the clouds. The FAC that they were working with saw him eject, but his parachute did not open fully. His wingmen searched for him until nightfall. His body was found the next day.

As the Vietnam contingent of the 185th Tactical Fighter Group was quickly going operational in Southeast Asia, the ones left back in Sioux City were being sliced and diced and thrown all over. Before the 174th Tactical Fighter Squadron and support personnel shipped overseas, Col. Donald W. Forney, the 185th's commander, presented his case for being included in the Vietnam force quite strongly, but much to his dismay he was denied. By the end of May, Forney was being sent to Cannon AFB, New Mexico. Reportedly, he stated that he was going to be the commander of the 140th Tactical Fighter Wing, which had been relocated there from Buckley ANG Base, Colorado. His assistance in getting the 140th re-established in its new location was "successfully completed," and he returned to Sioux City June 13th. At that time he had no idea where he would be sent next.

Forney found out soon. On June 25th, it was announced that he was going to Kunsan AB, South Korea, where he would be the commander of a new tactical fighter wing that would be formed upon his arrival—the 354th. He left Sioux City July 2nd and arrived at Kunsan AB on the 6th. This was not Col. Forney's first trip to Korea. In the 1951 Korean War mobilization, he was stationed at Taegu AB, from which he flew 151 support missions in a C-47. Taking over for Forney as the 185th's commander was Lt. Col. Warren G. "Bud" Nelson. Col. Nelson's reign over the 185th would be short-lived, as he would leave July 23rd to become Forney's wing deputy commander of operations. After Col. Nelson's departure, Lt. Col. James A. Konopisos commanded a skeleton force looking after the facilities and equipment not taken to other bases.

Soon 140 more officers and airmen would follow. Five left Sioux City by commercial airliner in the late hours of July 8th. In the early hours of July 9th, the rest boarded a Frontier Airlines

1st Lt. Warren K. Brown's aircraft was hit by ground fire July 14, 1968. Lt. Brown ejected from his crippled aircraft, but his parachute apparently failed to fully deploy. (*185th TFG/McCallum collection*)

Col. Donald W. Forney, who had been the commander of the 185th TFG, was assigned to Korea, where he commanded the 354th TFG at Kunsan AB. (*185th TFG/McCallum collection*)

Armament crew readying an F-100 for the next mission. (*185th TFG/McCallum collection*)

Boeing 727. Upon landing in Korea, they went to a number of bases. Some would join Colonels Forney and Nelson at Kunsan AB, while others went to Osan, Kwanju, Taegu, and Suwon Air Bases. Another 10 officers, seven of them pilots, and 154 airmen went to Cannon AFB in mid-July to be part of the 140th Tactical Fighter Wing. The seven pilots would be instructors in the FAC and combat crew training courses.

In June, the 174th received the additional duty of having two aircraft and crews standing 24-hour alert. With armed and loaded fighters, they would respond within 15 minutes to come to the aid of allied forces who found themselves in trouble. Captains John M. Haley and David S. Wilson were standing their shift on alert when the call came in that friendly forces had been ambushed and were pinned down near Ha Thanh. Making numerous passes at the enemy forces with intense automatic weapons fire, they delivered their ordnance on target. Their quick and accurate action relieved the pressure on the friendlies and enabled them to take charge of the situation.

Communications of accommodation came from all quarters. One from Col. Robert E. Archer, commanding officer of the 2nd Brigade, 9th Infantry Division, went like this:

> One battalion of army troops were airmobile into a rice paddy and immediately received intense enemy fire. The enemy was so well fortified that helicopter gunships and artillery could not suppress them.

Capt. John M. Haley. (*185th TFG/McCallum collection*)

Capt. Edward J Haerter. (*185th TFG/McCallum collection*)

Capt. David S. Wilson. (*185th TFG/McCallum collection*)

> The [174th] reacted with amazing speed when called upon to soften the Viet Cong positions. With complete disregard for their personal safety, the pilots delivered their ordnance with precise accuracy and inflicted heavy damage on the enemy force.
>
> My brigade will always look forward to working with your unit.

On this rescue mission to free up the battalion were: Maj. Robert C. Eybers, Capt. Edward J. Haerter, Capt. John M. Haley, Capt. Robert W. Ray, and 1st Lt. Lyle L. Bainbridge. On this flight Major Eybers was carrying the Iowa state flag, which was passed to another 174th pilot at the completion of the mission.

The U.S. Marines also got some help. A Marine recon team was operating in the middle of a horseshoe. They had problems with Viet Cong forces for a couple of nights, and on the third night got assistance from a couple of USAF fighters. The fighters worked

1st Lt. Lyle L. Bainbridge. Lt. Bainbridge was one of a number of 174th pilots to carry the Iowa state flag on a mission. (*185th TFG/ McCallum collection*)

over the area from which the Marines were taking fire. About two hours later things heated up again. Once again, air support was requested. Two F-100s under the call signs Bat 3 and Bat 4 showed up. On their first run they put their napalm 40 meters from the target. After that, each succeeding pass was on the target. This action was taking place at night, with parachute flares from a Marine helicopter throwing strange shadows all over.

After expending their ordnance, they strafed the area with their 20 mm cannons. The Marines observed that each strafing run was right on line with the targeted area in the tree line along the river, and started and ended perfectly. The Marine helicopter went in to make a bomb damage assessment. The Marines, which included the unit's executive officer, gave the fighters 100% for bombs on target and 100% for coverage of target. The executive officer stated that he had seen bombing as good but none better. The Marines radioed the fighters their thanks for the good work. One of the fighter pilots replied, "Thank you; you can depend on your Air National Guard."

Things were dangerous all over. On September 22nd, a flight of 174th F-100s took off from Phu Cat lead by Major Patrick C. Parks. About four minutes after takeoff, the F-100 flown by 1st Lt. Kuldar Visnapuu sustained heavy damage from ground fire. Major Parks checked Lt. Visnapuu's damaged aircraft and reported that he was streaming fuel. Visnapuu informed Parks that he was going to make the South China Sea and put his plane down there. Unfortunately, as he was approaching the sea coast he was down to 2,000 feet altitude and his speed had decreased to about 200 knots. It was time to eject.

1st Lt. Kuldar Visnapuu and his F-100 "Hombre." Lt. Visnapuu was hit by ground fire and was able to bail out. He was picked up almost immediately after landing by a U.S. Army helicopter. (*185th TFG/ McCallum collection*)

The lieutenant landed on the beach; he saw his craft crash about 100 yards offshore. He was uninjured, and was picked up almost immediately by a U.S. Army helicopter and taken back to Phu Cat AB.

Throughout their time in Vietnam, the aircrews were impressing the regulars of all the services with their proficiency and professionalism, their *esprit de corps*. But this was not only true of the pilots, but of all the enlisted, as well as the officers. No better place could this attitude be found than in the maintenance personnel. In many ways, the Air Guard proved to be of higher skill. Part of this can be attributed to the fact that the guard members had been associated with the same aircraft for many more years than the regulars. Quite often you could see Airmen Second and First Class working on a plane with a Staff Sergeant supervising. In the Air Guard, including the 174th, you saw Airmen First Class with Staff and Technical Sergeants working

Major Patrick C. Parks. (*185th TFG/McCallum collection*)

All the174th TFS F-100s carried the HA tail code. (*185th TFG/ McCallum collection*)

on a plane. There was also the fact that the Air Force was flying the F-100D, while the Guard had the F-100C. There was enough of a difference between the two to cause problems. Originally at Phu Cat AB, the personnel in the Phase Docs were to pull the tail off of their F-100Cs and the engine shop would then send their troops out to remove the engine. With the differences in hydraulics, structure, etc., the Air Force troops got into deep trouble in their attempts. Now, before the 174th left Sioux City, their Phase Doc people removed both the tail and engine on their planes, so the 174th Phase Doc supervisor relieved the regulars from their task and the 174th performed both functions from then on.

Lt. Col. Lloyd A. Pippett, of the 185th, was given the job of Maintenance Control Officer in the 37th Tactical Fighter Wing at Phu Cat AB. Every afternoon at 5:00 he would give the Chief of Maintenance the status of all four squadrons under the 37th. It got to the point that Col. LeRoy J. Manor, the 37th's commanding officer, only wanted to hear about the other three squadrons unless there was a real big problem. The 174th had such a good in-commission rate that they met all their requirements.

There was also a standard Wednesday morning meeting at 9 o'clock, where such things as hung bombs, aborts, and drag chute failures were discussed. The Iowans had been at Phu Cat for two to three months when the subject was drag chute failures. The F-100Cs of the 174th and the Air Force's F-100Ds utilized a drag chute to slow them down. The Air Force Ds had flaps to assist them in slowing

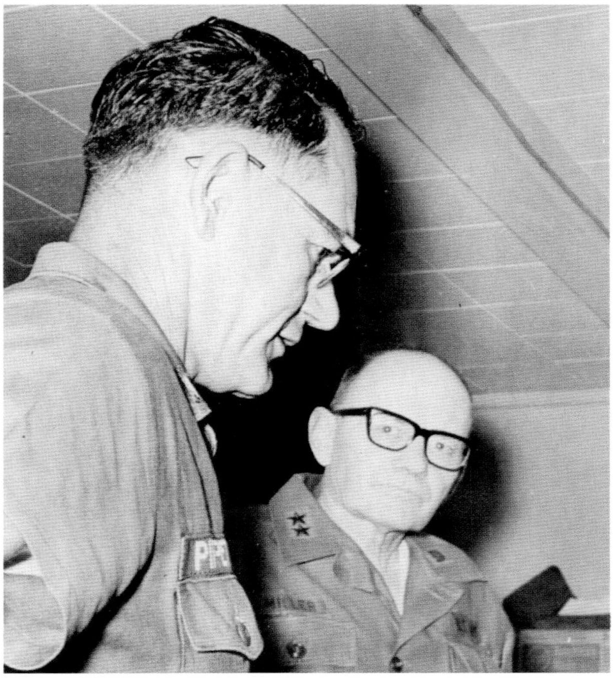

Lt. Col. Lloyd A. Pippett had commanded the 185th Consolidated Aircraft Maintenance Squadron in Iowa, but when he arrived in Vietnam he was assigned as the 37th TFW's Maintenance Control Officer. The ex-185th maintenance troops from Colonel Pippett on down were given great responsibility at Phu Cat. Pictured with Pippett is Iowa Adjutant General, Maj. Gen. Junior F. Miller. (*185th TFG/McCallum collection*)

down, but the Cs did not. The flaps helped reduce the landing speed. The D models landed at 155 knots, where the C model landed at about 183 knots. So Col. Pippett asked Col. Manor at this particular meeting if he could ask Manor a question. Manor obligingly said yes. Pippett's question was something like: "Why do the Ds have drag chute failure and run into the barrier on a regular basis and the Cs do not?" Pippett then left the room. It was reported that there was a "major chewing out" that followed.

There was musical talent among the Sioux City troops, including the Phu Cat Six. This was a six-piece band, of which half were from the Iowa contingent. Capt. Darrell F. Lake played the clarinet, Sgt. Jeff Watt the guitar, and Sgt. William Grainer was on the drums. In December 1968, they played for entertainer Bob Hope when he came to Phu Cat. They also enjoyed the view of actress Ann Margaret from their stage top position. They also had a singer/song writer, Capt. David S. Wilson. Capt. Wilson came up with lyrics for a couple of tunes, one of which was "Sweet Betsy of Pike." The first few lines went:

Maintenance was a never-ending process. The Sioux City troops maintained a high, even the highest, ready rate among the Phu Cat units. (*185th TFG/McCallum collection*)

Oh do you remember the call sign of Bat,
in South Vietnam at a base called Phu Cat.
Where we launch Super Sabres by day
and by night, with wall-to-wall high drags
we blast out of sight.

Capt. Jerry Edwards was a tall, lanky farmer from near Sergeant Bluff, Iowa. Known as "Big Ed," he had to have a cigarette as soon as his F-100 was shut down after a mission. In September, he volunteered to fly with the 416th Tactical Fighter Squadron, Misty, and was put on temporary duty with them that month. Between September 14, 1968, and January 11, 1969, Major Edwards flew 61 sorties in the F-100F.

By late August, the 174th had been averaging 24 sorties per day from the time they arrived in country. Leading the squadron in missions and flight hours at that time were Capt. Robert A. Anderson, Capt. David S. Wilson, and 1st Lt. John W. McClellan, with 73 missions and 115 combat flying hours each. By November, 14 of the 174th's pilots had joined the "Sabrejet" club. This meant that they had flown 1,000 hours in the F-100. A few more 174th pilots were just weeks away from attaining this distinction.

Capt. Jerry Edwards. Not only did Captain Edwards fly 174th missions, but he got himself temporarily assigned to the 416th TFS, the Misty squadron, and flew those very dangerous missions. *(185th TFG/McCallum collection)*

1969 would see a death for the 174th Tactical Fighter Squadron, plus an additional one of a stateside member of the 185th Tactical Fighter Group. At Phu Cat AB, Sgt. Harold P. Berg was assisting in weapons loading operations February 28th. He apparently fell from a tractor-drawn trailer that was being used in the loading operation. He was taken to the hospital, but died the following Monday, March 3rd, from an acute blood clot on the brain. MSgt. Gerald Kratochvil was mobilized with the 185th Tactical Fighter Group in January 1968. He decided to make the Air Force his career and reenlisted on February 10, 1969. One week later he died from a cerebral hemorrhage and a stroke while in the hospital.

In 1969, the 174th lost their third F-100C and almost a second pilot. 1st Lt. Clive J. Grewell, flying his 221st mission, and another pilot were working with Capt. Troy C. Usher, a FAC pilot flying an O-2A Super Skymaster in the bleak hill country in the Central Highlands of South Vietnam. Upon Capt. Usher's direction, the two F-100s made their first bombing runs with the aid of a smoke rocket that Capt. Usher had fired marking the area to be hit. After further directions from the FAC, the two Super Sabres made another run. The first fighter dropped his ordnance on the target area. Lt. Grewell was next, but he felt a hard thud and his fighter shuddered. Capt. Usher observed a part of Grewell's fighter fall away, followed by a small explosion. Lt. Grewell was able to bail out, but he found himself dazed, with a broken arm, and in unfriendly territory. Capt. Usher radioed for rescue assistance and immediately tried to contact Grewell. They made contact and the FAC located his position. Soon an Army HU-1E helicopter arrived on the scene. With the trees and brush in the area, the HU-1E first lowered a rope with a loop in it to haul the injured pilot up. Unfortunately

Capt. Robert A. Anderson. (*185th TFG/McCallum collection*)

Capt. John W. McClellan. (*185th TFG/McCallum collection*)

Grewell was having trouble, feeling faint as they were raising him, so he had them lower him to the ground in fear that he might lose consciousness, slide through the loop of rope, and fall to his death. That brave helicopter crew managed to land, get Lt. Grewell onboard, and flew him to an Army Evacuation Hospital at Pleiku AB.

All missions were not solely 174th affairs. Between February 28th and March 31st, Operation Iron Mountain was taking place along the Song Tra Khue River, south and west to the Song Re River in Quang Ngai Province. This was a clear and search operation by the 11th Infantry Brigade. On one of the support missions, the 37th Tactical Fighter Wing sent out a number of F-4s and F-100s to destroy a fortified enemy location. The battle damage assessment stated that 19 fortifications and a bunker were destroyed, which in turn touched off a secondary explosion. Major Patrick C. Parks and Capt. Robert A. Anderson of the 174th participated

1st Lt. Clive J. Grewell is presented a medal by Maj. Gen. Junior F. Miller. Grewell had his F-100 shot out from under him, but was recovered by the heroics of a rescue helicopter crew. (*185th TFG/ McCallum collection*)

in the mission. On another mission, Capt. Darrell E. Lake of the 174th, which was under the 37th Tactical Fighter Wing, flew with two pilots from the 31st Tactical Fighter Wing out of Tuy Hoa AB (where ex-ANG fighter squadrons from New Mexico and New York were stationed).

Early in the year, plans were taking shape regarding the Air Guard units being returned to their respective states. On February 6th, the National Guard Bureau authorized Iowa to form the 185th Provisional Detachment at Sioux City. Lt. Col. James A. Konopisos, who was commander of the skeleton crew maintaining what was left of the 185th, would be commander of the 185th Provisional Detachment. The purpose of the Detachment was to prepare for the return of the 185th Tactical Fighter Group personnel who had been scattered all over the world. Some would return in large groups, like the 174th and its support personnel, and those from Korea. Others would return over time, either individually or in small groups. Until they were returned officially to the state and the 185th Tactical Fighter Group was re-established, they would be assigned to the Detachment.

May 12th was the magic date, the going home day. But the 174th did not slack off; no "short timer" attitude there. They flew missions up to the last. They continued to have over 98% sortie effective rate, the highest Operational Ready rates in the 37th Tactical Fighter Wing. Out of the four squadrons then under the 37th, they had the best low dud rate (munitions that did not explode). They took part in a number of major operations: Khe Sanh, Dak To, Ben Het, Chu Lai, Duc Lap, and the A Shau Valley. By March 1969, they had flown more than 6,400 sorties and over 11,500 hours of combat flying.

It is reported that after the final mission Major Jerry Edwards thought, "Well, that's the end of that!" By this time they were not only the 174th Tactical Fighter Squadron, they were the Bats!

Landed at Phu Cat AB for the last time. Next flight—home. (*185th TFG/McCallum collection*)

Lt. Col. James A. Konopisos (this is an earlier photo) commanded a skeleton crew back at Sioux City and orchestrated all the necessary actions for the troops' return home. (*185th TFG/McCallum collection*)

Time to relax and celebrate. (*185th TFG/McCallum collection*)

Chapter Nine

Returning Home

Col. LeRoy J. Manor, commander of the 37th Tactical Fighter Wing at Phu Cat AB, Vietnam, wrote a letter of appreciation to Maj. Gen. Junior F. Miller, Iowa Adjutant General, in April 1969, as the 174th Tactical Fighter Squadron was completing their tour of duty:

> Throughout its combat tour, the 174th Squadron maintained the highest squadron in-commission rate, as well as the lowest abort rate in the wing; and at times, the 174th was tasked to fly more than its share of the daily operational commitments. During this period, the 174th Squadron accomplished more than 10,000 accident-free flying hours. This is especially noteworthy, in that nearly all of the sorties flown by the 174th involved heavy weight takeoffs, carrying and delivering all types of conventional ordnance in a hostile and hazardous combat environment. A large number of these missions required air refueling at high aircraft gross weight. With these outstanding accomplishments, the personnel of the 174th Squadron distinguished themselves as "professional airmen."

The 174th was given a good sendoff from Phu Cat. There was an awards ceremony, where some of their well-earned medals were presented. The squadron was also presented a 37th Tactical Fighter Wing flag, along with a "Job Well Done" plaque to take back to their Sioux City base. As a treat, the enlisted men enjoyed a picnic prepared for them. The officers were given a buffet supper. The 174th and their support personnel departed from Phu Cat, Vietnam, May 12, 1969, with quite a record. They, as well as the other Air National Guard fighter squadrons that served in Vietnam, can be credited with a major shift in Air Force thinking towards the Air Guard.

In May 1969, not only the 174th, but most of the 185th Tactical Fighter Group was on its way back home to Sioux City. On Wednesday, May 7th, an Air Force C-141 Starlifter arrived at Sioux City with Air Force personnel and equipment to in-process returning 185th. Another C-141 arrived on Thursday evening. Two returning airmen were expected to be on that flight, but only returning equipment was onboard. At 15 minutes after midnight, in the early morning hours of Saturday, May 10th, a large Air Force C-141 landed at Sioux City with almost 50,000 pounds of equipment and 33 Air Guardsmen of the 174th. Lt. Col. Lloyd A. Pippett, in charge of this contingent, was met by Lt. Col. James A. Konoposis, 185th Provisional Detachment commander, at Sioux City, as well as other Air Guardsmen of the welcoming committee.

In the 1960s, there was deep disdain amongst the American population. Our returning brave, battle-weary troops were shamefully greeted and treated, or ignored to a great extent. This was not the case for Sioux City. What the airmen found was a large "Welcome Home 185th Tac Ftr Gp" banner. As each man stepped off the C-141 and touched American soil for the first time in a year, they were given a welcome home present—a beer courtesy of the Sioux City beer distributors. As they exited from the air transport, they were not met by jeers and spit, as so many were at that time, but by cheers from sweethearts, wives, parents, and friends, who did not let barricades keep them from their loved ones. On the way home, the returning troops were treated to the sight of welcome home signs, American flags, and other patriotic symbols adorning the yards along the way.

The winds, gusting to 45 miles per hour, did not dampen the excitement of the first planeload of returnees. About two hours later, a commercial airline Boeing 707 brought another 163 members of the 174th back to Sioux City. By the time the 707 arrived, the temperature had dropped 16 degrees to a bone-chilling 49°. As one of the airmen remarked as he disembarked, "Damn, its cold." They too received a great welcome, including a beer. For the weeks to come, additional planes of equipment would be arriving, as well as the single airmen and small groups that had been stationed throughout the continental United States.

Then they saw it: a flight of six F-100s flying in perfect tight formation over Sioux City airport/ Air National Guard Base. Led by their commander, Lt. Col. Gordon L. Young, the fighters did a pitch-out formation and landed at five second intervals about a half mile apart. It was 5:45 in the afternoon of Wednesday, May 14th, and the cheers and tears of the large crowd awaiting the flyers were in full force. Col. Young, flying a two-place F-100F, led six F-100Cs in the first formation to leave Phu Cat. The planes made rest stops in Guam and Hawaii, with a lot of air refueling on the way. After leaving Guam, John Haley experienced problems and had to land at Wake Island. A maintenance crew was being sent in, but the fix wouldn't be soon, so Captain John M. Haley hopped a ride to Hawaii, where he joined Col. Young and got a ride in the F-100F. In the other F-100Cs were Capt. Darrell E. Lake, Capt. Sherman H. Sawin, Maj. Jerry Edwards, and Capt. Gordon W. Goodier. As with the airmen returning earlier in transport aircraft, the fighter pilots had the same large welcoming committee, plus Brig. Gen. Walter E. Williams, commander of the 140th Tactical Fighter Wing, which the 185th would fall under again, and others.

A second group arrived 30 minutes later. This group included Maj. Shirley M. Watson, Capt. Robert A. Anderson, Capt. Ronald G. Heitritter, and Capt. John W. McClellan, Jr. Because a number of 174th pilots had already returned, two of the pilots in this group were from New Jersey's 119th Tactical

May 14, 1969, was homecoming day for the 174th TFS. Here the F-100s have landed, but others will arrive by air transport. The crowds of greeters hung around to welcome all home. (*185th TFG/ McCallum collection*)

With the F-100F in the background, Lt. Col. Gordon L. Young is interviewed by the news media. (*185th TFG/McCallum collection*)

Pilots still in their F-100s; they will soon be welcomed by loved ones. The artistic side of the 174th came out in Vietnam. Names and artwork had been added since their departure from Sioux City. (*185th TFG/McCallum collection*)

Fighter Squadron, and had volunteered to serve in the 355th Tactical Fighter Squadron at Phu Cat (also under the 37th Tactical Fighter Wing). Next was a flight of four F-100s piloted by Maj. Dudley P. Smidt, Capt. Kuldar Visnapuu, Capt. Robert W. Ray, and another New Jersey Air Guardsman. The last flight of fighters arrived at 7:05 that evening, again a flight of four: 1st Lt. William W. Bowen, Maj. Patrick C. Parks, 1st Lt. Charles J. Blumer, and Lt. Col. Warren G. Nelson. These flights all received the same welcome as the first. It was a busy afternoon and evening, as C-141s continued to arrive with more returning guardsmen and equipment.

Col. Donald W. Forney, who had been the 185th Tactical Fighter Group's commander at the time of mobilization and subsequently assigned to Korea, where he was 354th Tactical Fighter Wing commander, was not scheduled to return to Sioux City until mid-June. His wing deputy commander of operations in Korea, Lt. Col. Warren G. Nelson, would become the 185th's acting commander May 27th. With Forney's delay in returning because of 354th duties, Col. Nelson went to Phu Cat and flew one of the 174th's F-100s back with the squadron.

The final large contingent of the 185th arrived at 3 o'clock in the morning, Saturday, May 17th, by chartered United Air Lines DC-8 airliner. Nearly 150 airmen found themselves welcomed by a crowd of around 500. Cold and windy, they were served hot coffee by the Red Cross, for which

Capt. John W. McClellan receives a very warm welcome by his family. (*185th TFG/McCallum collection*)

they were grateful. Col. Konopisos met this group, as he did all the others. He projected that all the guardsmen that had been stationed in the continental United States and returning individually or in small numbers would be back in Sioux City by midnight, Sunday, May 18th.

If the welcome the troops received at the airport upon their arrival home is considered quite spectacular for the 1960s, the parade they were given on Saturday, May 24th, was out of this world. Iowa governor Robert D. Ray proclaimed that day to be "Recognition Day" for the 185th Tactical Fighter Group. In Sioux City, it was "Recognition Day for the 185th." Thousands lined Nebraska Street, where an Army color guard, the Strategic Air Command band from Offutt AFB, Nebraska, local high school bands, floats, marching Army and Navy reserve units all participated, with the 174th pilots riding in convertible automobiles. Dignitaries from Sioux City, the state, and generals from the Air Force and National Guard were all there. After the parade, a barbecue and entertainment were provided for the

At 3 o'clock in the morning, the troops exiting off this United Airlines DC-8 didn't really care that it was cold and windy. The welcome they received warmed them up thoroughly. (*185th TFG/ McCallum collection*)

The banner says it all. All of Sioux City and the area around it seemed to turn out for their returning heroes. (*185th TFG/McCallum collection*)

returned airmen and their families at the Municipal Auditorium, where about 2,000 attended. Before Vietnam, some doubters voiced the opinion that, "It would never work when the chips are down." Brig. Gen. Walter E. Williams, of the 140th Tactical Fighter Wing, summed it up quite succinctly: "The 185th does not have to take a back seat to any group stationed in Vietnam, including the regular Air Force."

The returned airmen of the 185th had been spending time at home with their families, loved ones, and friends. On Monday, May 26th, they reported in at the Air Guard hangar at Sioux City airport to process in and prepare to be Air Guardsmen again. The following day, Lt. Col. Warren G. "Bud" Nelson became acting commander of the 185th. That Tuesday, all were in formation in the Air Guard Hangar for a change of command ceremony and demobilization. Many colonels and generals were looking on as the 185th was returned to the state of Iowa.

For the 1960s, this was quite a sight. (*185th TFG/McCallum collection*)

The processing back. "Hurry up and wait" is a common refrain in the military. It might even date back to General George Washington and his troops. (*185th TFG/McCallum collection*)

Maj. Gen Jay T. Robbins, 12th Air Force commander, presents a Distinguished Flying Cross medal that was awarded to Lt. Warren K. Brown posthumously to Brown's son, Troy. (*185th TFG/McCallum collection*)

The 174th Tactical Fighter Squadron had amassed quite a good record during its twelve months in Vietnam. As of February, they had destroyed or damaged 1,128 fortifications, 1,179 bunkers, and 21 sampans. They also set off 165 explosions and 269 fires. They killed some 486 enemy personnel. Their awards lay testament to their professionalism and skill as military aviators. As a unit, the Bats were awarded the Air Force Outstanding Unit Award and the Presidential Unit Citation. They were a great contributing factor in the 37th Tactical Fighter Wing being awarded the Southeast Asia Outstanding Fighter Wing Award. Individually, they were awarded (the count at the time they returned stateside) 12 Silver Stars (third highest medal), 35 Distinguished Flying Crosses, 30 Bronze Star medals, 115 Air Force Commendation Medals, some 300 Air Medals, and one Purple Heart.

During the change of command ceremony six awards (including the Silver Star medal, Distinguished Flying Cross, and Purple Heart) were posthumously awarded to Lt. Warren K. Brown. Gen. Jay T. Robbins, 12th Air Force commander, presented the awards to Lt. Brown's seven year old son, Troy, and his wife, Patricia. Today Major Troy Brown, who served in Operation Desert Storm and the Gulf War, is a retired Air Guardsman. During the change of command ceremony, and later during the August weekend drill, many more medals were awarded.

May 27, 1969, was quite a day at the Air National Guard base. All were present for the change of command ceremony and demobilization. They were once again part of the Iowa Air National Guard. (*185th TFG/McCallum collection*)

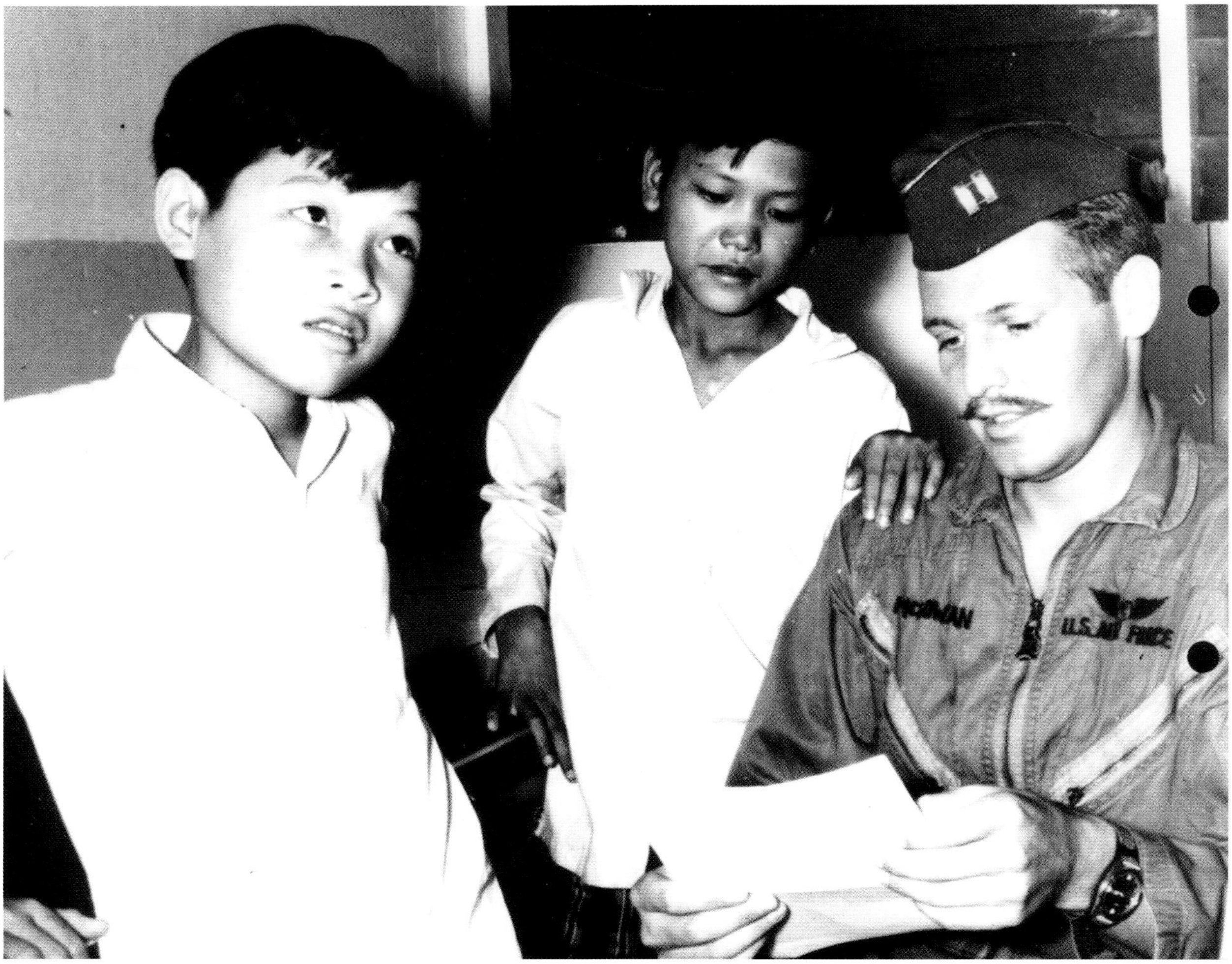

Capt. Gerald J. McGowan, 174th's flight surgeon, giving aid at the local Vietnamese orphanage. (*185th TFG/McCallum collection*)

The 174th also showed their humanitarian side while at Phu Cat AB. The 174th's flight surgeon, Capt. Gerald J. McGowan, set up a medical dispensary outside the base gate. Here he worked with Vietnamese doctors and nurses, training them in modern medical methods and bringing aid to the area villagers. He spent his days off and any spare time working in the dispensary with other 174th medical personnel. Other personnel aided in both Protestant and Catholic services at the base chapel. Others helped at the Kim Chau orphanage, located some 10 miles from the base. The airmen found the needs so great that they wrote friends, TV and radio stations, and newspapers back home for help. By Christmas 1968, they had received more than 300 boxes of gifts. Dr. McGowan requested and received medical supplies for the orphanage from his fellow doctors back home. The response was such that he was able to provide supplies to the Qui Hoa leprosarium, near Qui Non, and to the refugee center at Phu Cat village.

No matter where the Sioux City Air Guardsmen were sent, they were found to be capable and professional, and were considered value added to the war effort. The statistics are quite impressive. The 185th Tactical Fighter Group, including the 174th Squadron, as well as support squadrons, numbered 796 in total at the time of callup. Of that, 354 went to Phu Cat AB, Vietnam. That contingent, the largest, numbered 30 officers (25 of them pilots) and 324 enlisted personnel. In Korea, 16 officers (two were pilots) and 159 enlisted personnel were spread

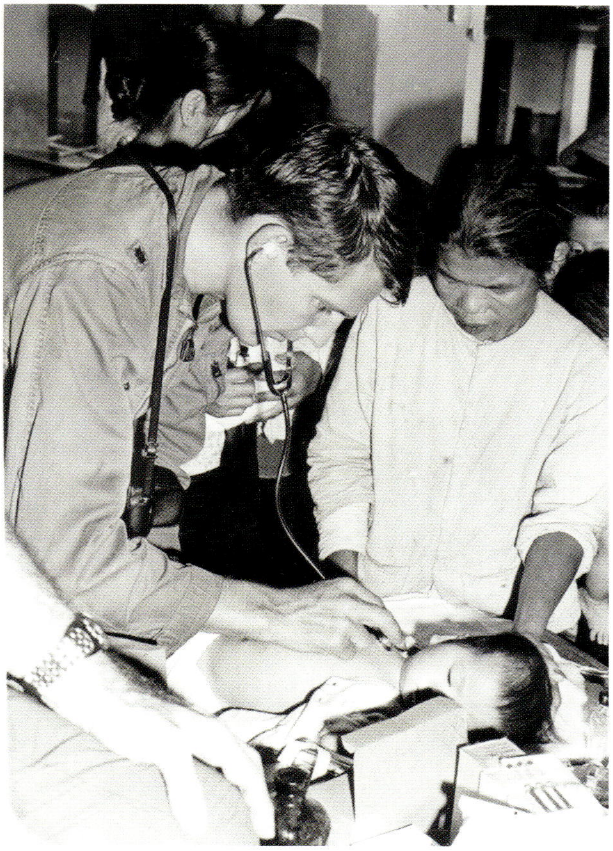

Maj. (Dr.) Gerald J. McGowan and Sgt. Thomas M. Burke providing health care to Vietnamese children. (*185th TFG/McCallum collection*)

between Kunsan AB, Osan AB, Kwanju AB, Taegu AB, and Suwon Air Base. Col. Donald W. Forney was commander of the 354th Tactical Fighter Wing at Kunsan AB, where Lt. Col. Warren G. Nelson was his deputy wing director of operations. They were the only 185th pilots in Korea. The 354th had major support problems, because its support units had been stripped for regular Air Force organizations. The F-100Cs and pilots were from two Air Guard squadrons that rotated personnel. The Air Force did not have F-100C support systems, so it was an effort for the 354th to keep their aircraft operationally ready. Maj. Richard J. Marx was the lone officer assigned to the island of Taiwan.

The theory before the call-up was that Air National Guard units, especially those manned, trained, and equipped under the Beef Broth/Combat Beef program, were to be deployed as a unit. What happened to the 185th, especially within the Continental U.S., just blows that theory away. Thirty officers, seven of them pilots, and 210 enlisted men were distributed over 33 Air Force bases in 21 states. The largest portion went to Cannon AFB, New Mexico, including ten officers (seven being pilots) and 154 airmen. The pilots that went to Cannon AFB were Maj. Charles R. Bradley, Capt. Jon P. Haddock, Capt. Ronald F. Lenagh, Capt. Donald A. Lundvall, Capt. John M. Miller, Capt. Bruce M. Mosier, and Maj. Norman D. Schaap. They served as instructor pilots in the 140th Tactical Fighter Wing combat crew and FAC training program. They flew quite a lot in an armed trainer called the AT-33. Captains Haddock and Lenagh spent some time at Davis-Monthan AFB, Arizona, as test pilots on a F-86 program, which was cancelled due to engine problems.

A good example of the enlisted man's plight, especially those spread all over the Continental U.S., was Technical Sergeant Duane E. "Mac" McCallum. When the 185th was mobilized, the orders stated that it could be for up to two years duration. Sergeant McCallum was quite busy when the call-up came. He almost immediately went from a one-man photo lab to 11, which included an Information Service Office and a graphics department. Soon they were being spread to Vietnam, Korea, and across the U.S. McCallum got orders for Mountain Home AFB, Idaho. Thinking it would be for two years, he packed his bags and family and moved. Fortunately, he found himself in charge of a photo lab for a squadron of tactical reconnaissance aircraft. His experience with the 174th as a Tactical Reconnaissance Squadron

The Air National Guard base in the early 1970s. Many of the buildings shown no longer exist. The countryside is not as open any longer, either. (*185th TFG/McCallum collection*)

flying RF-84Fs really paid off. He had expertise and experience that was much appreciated by "the regulars," who had been struggling with that task. He was rewarded by the "regulars," promoting him to Master Sergeant.

May ended in Sioux City with a monument dedicated to Lt. Warren K. Brown in the parking lot of that city's large Bella Hess Superstore on the 30th. Today the monument stands proudly at the entrance of Sioux Gateway Airport/Col. Bud Day Field terminal entrance. The final step in the return of the 185th Tactical Fighter Group back to Iowa occurred June 14th, when Col. Donald W. Forney arrived back home from his assignment as 354th Tactical Fighter Wing commander in Korea. Five days later he once again commanded the 185th.

When discharged from federal service, many Air Guardsmen had fulfilled their military obligation, similar to what happened back in 1953, when the 174th Fighter-Bomber Squadron was demobilized from the Korean call-up and had to reform again. Now, after the Vietnam mobilization, the 174th Tactical Fighter Squadron, as well as the 185th Group, had to rebuild their organizations.

In mid-November 1969, the markings of war are still visible on the F-100s. (*185th TFG/McCallum collection*)

The Warren K. Brown memorial was dedicated May 30, 1969, in Sioux City's large Bella Hess Superstore parking lot. Today it stands proudly at the Sioux Gateway Airport/Col. Bud Day Field near the terminal building. (*185th TFG/McCallum collection*)

From the inception of the Air National Guard after World War II it was, and continues to be even today, a struggle for funding, as well as modern equipment. From the Korean War through the Vietnam War, the capability and expertise of the Air Guardsmen improved to the point that they were on par with the regulars, especially the tactical fighter squadrons sent to Vietnam. Integration within the USAF was a somewhat choppy affair, and at times over the years on slippery footing. The integration of the Air Guard and the Air Force can be traced back to the 1950s and the runway alert program. This was followed by the gaining command concept and boosted by Beef Broth/Combat Beef. Energized by a Rand Corporation study in the late 1960s, the Total Force concept was put into action in 1970 under Air Force Regulation 45-1, "Purpose, Policy, and Responsibilities for Air National Guard and Air Force Reserve." To a good extent, because of President Johnson's reluctance to call up reserve forces and depend on the draft, and the public outcry that resulted, this regulation states that the reserve forces would "be the initial and primary source" for augmenting the regular forces, and that they would "perform peacetime missions as an adjunct

By 1971, the names and artwork had been removed from the noses of the squadron's F-100s. Also, the last three digits of the planes' serial numbers has been added to the vertical stabilizer in large white numerals. (*185th TFG/McCallum collection*)

Keeping their skills honed, a pilot of the 174th drops a bomb over a bombing range. (*185th TFG/McCallum collection*)

to, or corollary of, training." This would see the 185th Group and its 174th Squadron get more modern equipment and greater responsibility over the next decades. There would always be tension between the Air Guard and the Air Force when funding was minimized, and it would become a fight over who would suffer the loss of aircraft and/or units.

The need for replacements was anticipated as early as February 1969. At that time, the National Guard Bureau authorized the 185th to recruit around 150 non-prior service personnel. But by early 1970, the 185th had to scale back on non-prior service recruits due to budget cuts. In order to lure prior service noncommissioned officers to join the 185th, a "Try One" [year] enlistment program was started in February 1970. Through a direct commissioning program, 10 became commissioned officers. A number of replacement pilots were also needed. One, 1st Lt. Richard Fechter, received the Militiaman Award for being the number one graduate in his pilot training class. One of the pilots that opted not to reenlist after returning from Vietnam was Capt. Robert A. Anderson. After his discharge he moved to California, where he died of pneumonia October 30, 1969.

To maintain the 174th as a combat-ready squadron, additional or expanded facilities were needed. In the spring of 1970, a team from the 185th Civil Engineering Flight went to Whiteman AFB, Missouri. There they dismantled two B-58 Hustler alert hangars, transported them back to Sioux City, and erected them that fall at the Air National Guard Base at Sioux City Airport. They were erected just off the flight line. Additional space for the Engine Shop was needed. Funding was obtained, and construction was started in the spring of 1972.

In early 1971, the Sioux City Air Guard held a contest for a 185th Group emblem and for a new, modernized one for the 174th. Master Sergeant Grover Massey won for the Group's emblem, and 174th squadron commander Lt. Col. Gordon Young won for the Squadron's emblem. Both emblems were approved May 13, 1971.

At noon on April 24, 1972, all Iowa Army and Air National Guard vehicles and aircraft were grounded by Executive Order Number Eight of Iowa governor Robert D. Ray. The problem stemmed from an aircraft accident December 9, 1968. A 124th Fighter-Interceptor Squadron F-89J out of Des Moines was flying in the early evening. The crew consisted of pilot Capt. John H. Rooks and his radar operator, Lt. Larry L. Thomas. They crashed into the Follinglo Farmstead, which was located near Sioux City. The crash destroyed most of the buildings and the 1968 crop. In a three-year effort the Tjernagel family, which owned the farm, had not been compensated.

Then a Wisconsin Air Guard jet crashed on the farm of Clarence and Emma McCarville near Cresco,

In early 1971, the Sioux City air guard held a contest for the first group emblem and an updated one for the 174th TFS. MSgt Grover J. Massey's design won for the 185th emblem, and Lt. Col. Gordon L. Young won the replacement design for the 174th. Both emblems were approved by the USAF May 13, 1971. (*185th TFG/McCallum collection*)

The 174th was soon settled in and back to normal operations from their war experience. Two-week summer training at Volk Field, Wisconsin, was probably a lot more comfortable than Phu Cat. (*185th TFG/McCallum collection*)

Ready for the next flight. They were not all military related. In 1972, one of the squadron's F-100s flew to Kansas City to pick up antivenom serum for a patient at the Plainview, Nebraska, hospital who had been bitten by a rattlesnake. Because the local airport in Nebraska could not accommodate the F-100 it flew to Sioux City, where the serum was transferred to a waiting twin-engine U-3A. (*185th TFG/McCallum collection*)

Iowa, destroying their home and all that was in it. The McCarvilles also had not been compensated by the Air Force. As these aircraft were on Air Force missions, Governor Ray grounded all National Guard aircraft and vehicles until the Air Force compensated the families. Ray's action prompted an immediate response and the two families were compensated. By Executive Order Number Nine, Governor Ray rescinded the grounding order April 25, 1972. The 174th Tactical Fighter Squadron was free to fly again.

Once again, the 185th Tactical Fighter Group flew a mercy mission. In June 1972, the Plainview General Hospital in Nebraska was in urgent need of rattlesnake anti-venom serum. The 185th flew one of its F-100Cs to Kansas City, where the serum was available, and brought it back to Sioux City. In Sioux City it was transferred to a twin-engine Cessna U-3A to be flown to Plainview airport.

The 174th Tactical Fighter Squadron continued to participate in exercises. Between November 29 and December 16, 1972, the U.S. Readiness Command out of McDill AFB, Florida, ran joint exercise Brave Shield III. The 174th participated, along with regular and reserve forces, both Army and Air. Exercises like Brave Shield III were designed to insure that the general purpose combat forces were ready when and if U.S. Readiness Command was directed by the Joint Chiefs of Staff to reinforce other U.S. unified commands.

Nurses had been allowed in the National Guard, Army and Air, since the 1950s. Congress authorized the enlistment of prior-service females in the Guard by Public Law 90-130 in 1967; the law was effective July 1, 1968. In 1971, PL 90-130 was amended to allow non-prior service females to enlist in the Guard. On July 1, 1972, A1C Vickie S. Hansen of Holstein, Iowa, was the first non-nurse

In the early 1970s, Air Guard F-100Cs were experiencing engine failures. Some of the failures resulted in the pilot being killed. At least three 174th pilots experienced engine related problems during this period. Fortunately, there were no serious injuries. (*185th TFG/McCallum collection*)

female to join the Sioux City unit. She had been in the supply career field in the Air Force and would continue in that field in the Air Guard. She would be followed almost two years later by the first non-prior service enlistees when, on May 18, 1974, two local high school seniors, Nancy R. Lundy and Susan L. Bremmer, joined the 185th.

The F-100Cs of the 174th Tactical Fighter Squadron were experiencing engine problems, which other units were also having. On July 11, 1970, Lt. Robert D. Brink was part of a flight of four F-100Cs on a routine low-level training mission when he experienced an engine flame-out. The lieutenant bailed out without injury. The plane crashed near Davenport, Nebraska. Almost a year later to the day, Capt. James R. Gorlinsky was killed when his F-100C crashed in South Dakota. That August, Jon W. McClellan, Jr. ejected safely from his F-100C as his plane crashed during summer encampment at Volk Field, Wisconsin. It crashed near Volk Gunnery Range. In late August 1972, Major David S. Wilson suffered a lower back injury when he ejected from his F-100C after an apparent engine failure. On October 21, 1970, Major Robert C. Eybers had completed a practice night air refueling and was landing when he had problems with the engine throttle and was not able to stop the aircraft. The craft went 1,160

During the year, the squadron would deploy to different bases for gunnery practice, the normal two-week summer training, and other exercises and competitions. (*185th TFG/McCallum collection*)

feet beyond the southeast end of the runway and through the approach lights that were there. Major Eybers had deployed his drag chute, but had missed catching the arresting barrier. An F-100 equipment review conference was held at the Sioux City ANG Base between September 26th and 29th, 1972. In the June 1973 issue of *National Guard Magazine*, the president of the National Guard Association of the United States, Maj. Gen. Henry W. McMillan, stated that "One serious deficiency affecting the Air National Guard is the fact that 21 of its Tactical Fighter Squadrons fly the 'outdated' F-100, with an unreliable engine and limited weapons capability."

The Middle East has been a hotbed of conflict for decades. The United States support of Israel during the October 1973 Arab-Israel War, known as the Yom Kippur War, infuriated the Arab states. To strike back at the U.S., the Arab members of the Organization of Petroleum Exporting Countries, known as OPEC, placed an embargo against the U.S. On November 1st, U.S. President Richard M. Nixon announced certain steps that were being taken by the federal government to conserve energy. Iowa Governor Robert D. Ray directed like measures to take effect November 9th in Executive Order Number Seventeen, which included the curtailment of all non-essential training missions of Air Guard aircraft. In early January 1974, the Federal Energy Office increased the amount of fuel the military could use, which allowed resumption of suspended 174th flights, as well as all Air Guard units. The Arab oil embargo, along with the wind down of activity from the U.S.'s disengagement from the Southeast Asia conflict, impacted Air Guard aircraft upgrades. Some Air Guard units only upgraded from one model to a newer model of aircraft. This would be the case of the 174th in 1974, as they went from the F-100C to the F-100D.

The F-100C was already out of the USAF when the 174th went to Vietnam. In the first half of the 1970s, it was showing its age. There was pressure coming from a number of places for the Air Force to replace the aging F-100Cs with A-7s in the Air National Guard inventory. For the 174th, this would not happen until 1977. (*185th TFG/McCallum collection*)

The 174th started its upgrade to the F-100D when the first aircraft arrived January 23, 1974. The last F-100C left Sioux City May 19th, and was flown to Eglin AFB, Florida, where it would become part of the Air Force Armament Museum. It was not the last of the 174th Super Sabres. The first F-100C the squadron received (tail number 005 on June 3, 1961) was staying on base as a gate guard memorial to the Bats of Vietnam.

Unfortunately, the F-100C slated for display would replace a unique aircraft, the RF-84K. When the 174th became a tactical reconnaissance squadron in 1958, they were equipped with Republic RF-84F Thunderflash aircraft, except for one RF-84K. In the early 1950s, the Air Force developed a program of B-36 bombers carrying parasite fighters/reconnaissance aircraft. In 1955, it went operational with the Strategic Air Command. The parasite reconnaissance that SAC used was a modified RF-84F designated the RF-84K. When SAC discontinued their use, the RF-84Ks were distributed among Air National Guard squadrons. The 174th received one. When the 174th changed to the F-100C they donated their sole RF-84K to the city of Sioux City. Unfortunately, the city found the upkeep of the aircraft, including problems with vandalism, was too much, and they gave it back to the Air Guard, who put it on display at the gate. This unique aircraft just could not find a home. When the Air Guard replaced it with the F-100C, the RF-84K was used in fire fighting practice and destroyed.

The biggest problem in transitioning from the F-100C to the D model was transitioning the unit's simulator. There was no replacement flight simulator available, so the 185th simulator and maintenance personnel, along with depot personnel from Hill AFB, managed to modify the one at Sioux City. It took five people six weeks to accomplish the program. The major difference between the two models of the F-100 was that the D had a sophisticated navigational avionics system. It also had flaps which the C model did not.

The 174th did get an aircraft upgrade in 1974, when the first of the squadron's F-100Ds arrived at Sioux City. The squadron would be equipped with sister F-100Ds like this one over the next few months. (*185th TFG/McCallum collection*)

What would become known as the Super Bowl blizzard struck the Midwest on the second weekend in January 1975. One of the worst snow storms in memory kept the 185th busy, as well as the Army National Guard, flying six helicopters to rescue stranded people and supplying feed and hay to farms in a thirty-county area around Sioux City. The Air Guard troops aided the Army helicopter operations, as well as operating two snowplows and other equipment in an effort to keep the airfield operational.

In May 1976, the North Atlantic Treaty Organization (NATO) planned exercise Dashing Impact 76 to test NATO plans for the defense of northeastern Italy. It also was designed to train personnel to handle external reinforcements in time of war. Participating were Air National Guard squadrons from Sioux City and Des Moines, Iowa, and Sioux Falls, South Dakota, along with USAF, Royal Air Force (Great Britain), the Italian Air Force, and U.S. Navy carrier-based units, as well as land forces. On May 6th, an earthquake measuring 6.5 on the Richter scale shook northeastern Italy. Aviano AB, where the fighters were to operate out of, was not damaged; the surrounding towns were severely damaged or destroyed. The Guardsmen had been put up in a number of hotels in Pordenone, which

This F-100D is sporting the then-newest Air National Guard emblem on its tail. (*185th TFG/McCallum collection*)

The end of an era, as the sun sets on the F-100. The F-100 had flown with the 174th for nearly 17 years. (*185th TFG/McCallum collection*)

sustained damage, but no Guardsmen were injured. Because of the severe damage in the area, the Italian government suspended all flying activities, except for those connected with the relief effort. The Guard mission suddenly turned to a rescue mission. In the second week the aircraft and maintenance personnel went to Ramstein AB, Germany, where flight training missions were undertaken.

A pair of 174th F-100Ds fly over Gulfport, Mississippi, on a training mission in early 1976. (*185th TFG/McCallum collection*)

The year ended for the 174th and its F-100s with participation in exercise Brave Shield XV at Tyndall AFB, Florida. The 185th sent 71 members, including some from the 174th, along with aircraft, to participate in this massive joint readiness exercise. The 174th pilots provided some of the close air support for the opposition ground forces. All branches of the military participated, totaling over 16,000 personnel.

Chapter Ten

The A-7 Comes to Siouxland

In a 1965 Rand study they suggested the A-7 for the Air Guard as a means of modernizing their tactical fighter role. Some eight years later, Iowa Senator Harold E. Hughes, a strong Air National Guard advocate, asked the Senate Armed Services Committee to push the Air Force to provide the Air National Guard with more modern aircraft like the A-7 Corsair II fighter-bomber, which was produced by Vought Corporation. In March 1976, it was announced that the 174th Tactical Fighter Squadron would be receiving the A-7D Corsair II. A new Aerospace Ground Equipment, or AGE, building was constructed in 1976, the first of a number of new buildings in preparation for the A-7 fighter-bomber. The first A-7D arrived December 15, 1976. A "Welcome to Iowa" ceremony was held upon its arrival, including representatives from federal, state, county, and municipal governments.

A change in aircraft was not the only change in the wind. Col. Donald W. Forney had joined the 174th when it was first formed in 1946. When the squadron returned to state control after the Korean mobilization, he was appointed commanding officer January 28, 1953. Then, when the 185th Group was formed October 1, 1961, he became the first Group commander. Now, with 26 years with the Sioux City Air Guard, he was moving up. On April 6, 1976, Col. Warren G. "Bud" Nelson took the reins of the 185th, while Col. Forney, soon to be Brig. Gen. Forney, moved to Des Moines, where he became Assistant Adjutant General for Air of the Iowa National Guard.

The F-100, both C and D models, flew with the 174th for nearly 16 years. The squadron had the C model for nearly 13.5 of the years, and a total of 40 different Cs over that time. At the time the last three Ds left for the Arizona bone yard May 17, 1977, Lt. Col. Sherman H. Sawin topped the list of flight hours in the F-100 with 3,382 hours. In those 16 years, three aircraft were lost in combat (one fatality), and there were 14 peacetime accidents/incidents with three pilots lost. The more severe accidents were usually related to engine problems.

The A-7 is slower than the F-100, but for the ground attack role it has a computerized navigational and weapons delivery system that makes it more effective. By the end of May 1977 all the F-100s were gone, and the squadron had 20 A-7Ds by the end of May, though they had already lost one of their new airplanes on April 7th. Major John Ahnert was on a training mission in Wisconsin when his engine failed and he was unable to restart it. Major

The first A-7D was received December 1, 1976, but it would be later in 1977 that the 174th would become operational. The A-7Ds would go through a number of paint schemes over the 15 years that the 174th would fly them. The A-7s were originally received with the light underside. (*185th TFG/McCallum collection*)

Emergency under control. (*185th TFG/McCallum collection*)

Ahnert successfully ejected from the crippled craft near Fort McCoy without injury.

The A-7 proved itself to be an excellent ground support aircraft in Vietnam. According to Vought Corporation, A-7D serial number 70-0930, which the 174th received, dropped the last bomb in the Vietnam War. Unfortunately, this aircraft would be lost March 25, 1979, when it experienced engine failure near Ewing, Nebraska, and Lt. Gary Cranmer had to eject.

Operation Snowbird was begun at Davis-Monthan AFB, near Tucson, Arizona, to give Air Guard units in heavy winter states a place to train between January and April in less severe climate. The 174th Tactical Fighter Squadron, along with maintenance personnel from the 185th Tactical Fighter Group, deployed to Davis-Monthan AFB January 21, 1978, for Snowbird training through February 4th. About 140 Sioux City Air Guardsmen, along with their new A-7s, went to Arizona on this deployment.

To reinforce the Total Force concept and indoctrinate the 185th Tactical Fighter Group in the Tactical Air Command's concept of deployment and combat readiness, the 185th conducted their summer encampment at Savannah Municipal Airport, Georgia, in 1978. Unfortunately, while on a simulated weapons delivery over Lake George, in northern Florida, Lt. Col. Jerry Edwards lost his life when his A-7 went into the lake.

The United States Southern Command, headquartered in Panama, was feeling the pinch, both from shrinking budgets and a low priority. They first requested Air National Guard and Air Force Reserve to assist in providing transport assistance. They started getting C-130 assistance from these units on a rotating basis in October 1977. Southern Command also had been getting the

In 1978, the two-week annual training was held in Savannah, Georgia. Here two of the 174th's are on the ramp in Savannah. (*185th TFG/McCallum collection*)

Under Coronet Cove, four A-7s from various Air Guard units were stationed at Howard AB, Panama. For a number of years, the 174th took its turn. Crew chiefs from the 174th are preparing their aircraft for the day's missions. (*185th TFG/McCallum collection*)

fighter protection of Tactical Air Command units since 1971, but that too had to be replaced by Air National Guard units.

Under Operation Coronet Cove, fourteen Air National Guard fighter squadrons and support units would send volunteers and full-time personnel to Howard AB, Panama. The 185th Tactical Fighter Group was one of the first to go. In September 1978, they sent their first group for two weeks, which included four A-7s. Support personnel flew down in a C-130. At the end of their tour a second group relieved them. Their mission was to provide fighter protection for the Canal Zone and support U.S. Army training exercises. Operation Coronet Cove lasted until the end of January 1990.

The Air Guard, like all military services, participated in activities called "operations" or "exercises" multiple times each year for training, honing their skills, practice working with much larger forces, and operating under combat conditions. Both the 174th squadron and at the larger 185th group

In formation over the farmlands of Iowa. (*185th TFG/McCallum collection*)

One of the two two-place A-7Ks assigned to the 174th. (*185th TFG/McCallum collection*)

level, the Sioux City Air Guard participated in these events a number of times per year. One of the big ones was the Red Flag exercises carried out at Nellis AFB, near Las Vegas, Nevada. The 185th sent over 200 personnel in 1979, and for a few years after. Operation Snowbird continued and, like the local civilians in the area that go to California and Arizona to escape the Midwest winters and are referred to as "snowbirds," the Sioux City Air Guard followed suit.

The pilots and support personnel were becoming world travelers. As mentioned above, trips to Panama for Operation Coronet Cove were a yearly occurrence for many years to come. Three of the pilots went to Germany for Operation Crested Eagle in February 1980. Closer to home, but still out of the country, they participated in Maple Flag VIII at the Canadian Forces Base located at Cold Lake, Medley, Alberta, Canada, in September 1981. Eighty-two personnel and six A-7s spent two weeks in this exercise, which was the Nellis Red Flag exercise equivalent. Here the Air Guard A-7s were pitted against the F-5s, F-101s, and F-104s of the Canadians.

One bit of good news that came down the chain of command in 1980 was that additional A-7Ds and two-place A-7Ks were coming into Air National Guard inventory. The 174th would have their operational aircraft inventory of A-7Ds increased to 24, and they would be getting two of the A-7Ks. Due to "delays," the squadron would not get its first A-7K until February 1, 1983. Another bit of news in 1980 concerning the A-7Ds was that they would be getting a new color scheme. In this scheme, the white underbelly was eliminated and it was painted in the "new Lizard color scheme." This meant the entire aircraft needed to be painted. The effort started in July.

One of the 174th's pilots, 1st Lt. Steve Powell, entered the Guiness Book of Records June 21, 1980. On that date he performed 2,311 inside loops. Though Lt. Powell was an A-7 pilot, he performed this feat on his own time and in a rented civilian aircraft in Almont, Michigan. The National Aeronautical Association certified that he had beaten the previous record of 1,501 inside loops.

An A-7 incident on September 23, 1980, helped to solve a fleet-wide problem. On that date, Capt. Richard Fechter was flying formation near Anoka, Nebraska, when his engine quit. He went through the standard engine restart procedures, but no luck. He was losing altitude, and his wingman advised him that it was time to eject. Capt. Fechter ejected. His craft was going slow enough and was fairly low, so that when it crashed, the engine and surrounding assemblies were in pretty good shape. The depot at Tinker AFB, Oklahoma, upon examination, found that a nut had backed off, which in turn caused fuel starvation. Upon checking other aircraft in the fleet, this problem was found and was traced to other aircraft having flameout problems like Capt. Fechter had experienced.

The 174th Tactical Fighter Squadron was formed in 1946 as the 174th Fighter Squadron, Single Engine. On December 31, 1982, the last two charter members of that original organization retired: Lt. Col. Richard J. Marx and CMS Robert D. Petrik.

Operation Sentry Partner was a different kind of exercise. It didn't involve the 174th pilots directly, but it did their wives. During the unit's August 1984 summer field training, 11 wives were able to ride along in an Illinois Air Guard KC-135 tanker and observe their husbands first hand performing aerial refueling high over the heartland of Iowa.

While Snowbirding at Davis-Monthan in January 1984, the 174th pilots participated in Dissimilar Air Combat Training (DACT). Here the A-7 pilots were pitted against F-5E and F-4D Aggressor aircraft. Simulating Soviet tactics, this gave the Iowa pilots experience in operating against aircraft of different sizes and tactics.

The 132nd Tactical Fighter Wing and its three groups, including the 185th, took part in what was the largest training Air National Guard deployment at the time. Between May 11 and June 8, 1985, thirty-six A-7s (12 from each group) flew to RAF Waddington, Lincolnshire, England. The non-stop flight, which included air refueling, took eight hours. All together 54 pilots, 900 support personnel, and some 66 tons of equipment made the journey. Called Operation Coronet Buffalo, the Air Guard pilots flew low level missions, air-to-air combat, air refueling, and gunnery at local ranges. They flew over the British Isles, Germany, the Netherlands, and other NATO countries. In this exercise, the unit's personnel experienced how it was to operate from bases overseas and learn NATO procedures.

A formation of 174th A-7s over the Sioux City ANG base in the 1980s. (*185th TFG/McCallum collection*)

Beginning in 1976, Operation Team Spirit was a joint exercise between U.S. Military Forces Korea and the South Korean military. It was both a training exercise, and a show of force and American resolve for the North Koreans. In the largest deployment since the Vietnam mobilization for the 185th Tactical Fighter Group, they dispatched 240 personnel, along with 12 A-7s, in March 1986 for Operation Team Spirit 86. This was a large exercise, with some 200,000 soldiers, sailors, and airmen.

They would be stationed at Kunsan AB, South Korea. Here operations were different. At Kunsan they practiced Aircraft Surge Launch and Recovery (ASLAR). In this method, more aircraft could be launched and recovered faster and in tighter configurations. The 185th Group and 174th Squadron pilots had to practice and perfect this technique prior to deployment.

On this exercise, Col. Gerald W. Swartzbaugh, the group commander, led the A-7 force to Korea. The pilots were billeted in Officer's quarters, but

A pair of A-7s in the gray paint scheme which started to appear in the early 1980s. (*185th TFG/McCallum collection*)

most of the rest of the troops were billeted in 32 by 16 tents, with nine men each. Each airman had a cot in a tent and was issued one electric plug and a smoke detector. It was raining when they arrived.

It was meant to simulate roughing it under wartime conditions, and it met all expectations. The pilots flew close air support missions with constant simulated threat of either ground or air attacks. For the two weeks, the personnel were under simulated chemical attack and had to wear or carry chemical warfare gear whenever they were out of the tent area. In one four-day period they had to wear the full gear for 10 hours.

Because of the 185th Tactical Fighter Group's exceptional record on three major inspections, flying and ground safety, and its outstanding record on support functions, it was awarded the Air Force Outstanding Unit Award. Brig. Gen. John D. Logeman, Vice Commander of Twelfth Air Force, presented the award in a ceremony in front of the Air Guard hangar June 7, 1986.

Training and simulated warfare seemed to take up all of 1988. It started in January, helping to train

A flock of A-7s with the always welcome KC-135 flying gas station. The squadron had no thought of them becoming an air tanker outfit in about 20 years. (*185th TFG/McCallum collection*)

Army ground Forward Air Controllers at Eglin AFB, Florida. Then the Sioux City Guardsmen went to St. Truiden, Belgium, where they participated in Crested Eagle 88 NATO exercises in March. In mid-July they flew to Spangdahlem AB, Germany, for Creek Corsair. August saw them back in Panama on Coronet Cove 88. October saw the Air Guardsmen back at Nellis AFB for another Red Flag exercise. But that was not the end for October. From Red Flag they went across the country to take part in Air Warrior II. Here the airmen flew close air support for a light infantry division at Little Rock, Arkansas.

Flight ramp full of A-7s. Fuel trucks and other vehicles are busy getting some of the aircraft ready for the day's missions. (*185th TFG/ McCallum collection*)

In 1989, the A-7 was showing its age. That year the 185th took top honors in Twelfth Air Force's Gunsmoke competition for A-7s. As the winner, they entered the Air Force's world-wide Gunsmoke competition. Here the A-7 was just outclassed by the modern F-16 fighters. But where the 185th could shine they did—maintenance. Here they won first place for A-7 maintenance and first place for best appearance of its planes.

Cracks were being found in the wings of A-7s. Using non-destructive inspection, 11 out of the 20 174th A-7s were found to have this problem. They were subsequently grounded, and were unable to

While on deployment in Germany, a 174th A-7 flies in formation with an RF-4 near a picturesque German castle. (*185th TFG/ McCallum collection*)

participate in deployments between June through August 1989.

United Airlines flight 232 left Denver, Colorado, at about 2:09 on the afternoon of July 19, 1989. They had been flying for about one hour and ten minutes when the number two engine blew and did the unthinkable—it took out the hydraulics, including the backup systems. Capt. Alfred C. Haynes, along with his flight crew (First Officer William Records and Second Officer Dudley Dvorak) and with the assistance of DC-10 instructor Dennis E. Fitch, who had been deadheading on the flight, used their combined knowledge and strength just to keep the crippled plane in the air and upright.

After the engine blew and they discovered they had no hydraulics, and could only control the aircraft by throttle manipulation, they contacted Air Traffic Control and declared an emergency. It was first suggested that they go to Des Moines airport, because Sioux Gateway airport was not classified for wide-bodied aircraft and did not have the emergency response units needed. But Des Moines was about 170 miles away and Sioux Gateway 70. With a 20-minute warning to the airport, 185th Tactical Fighter Group and Gary Brown of Sioux City Emergency Services all did what they had been trained to do in emergencies. Without worrying who was going to pay for what, surrounding communities were contacted and made part of the team from the beginning moments. Lookout vehicles were stationed along the countryside in the possible flight path between the DC-10's last reported location and the airport. This was done so the word could be given if the plane came down prior to the airport and emergency vehicles would know where to go.

The crippled DC-10 was aiming for runway 31. Emergency vehicles from the Air Guard, airport, and from Sioux City and surrounding communities were lining up on runway 22. Two minutes out, and the crew of 232 realized that they were not going to make runway 31; the plane was going to 22. Suddenly the emergency equipment and personnel had to scramble, fast!

The plane, which usually lands at 140 knots, hit the right wing tip, engine, gear, and the nose gear at about 215 knots. The right wing broke off, and with fuel spilling out, burst into a huge ball of fire. The rest of the plane slammed into the ground and went sliding (it didn't cartwheel) and broke apart, with parts of the fuselage rolling and ending up in a corn field. Between Guardsmen that were on base and those that rushed to the base, there were hundreds to assist. Col. Romaine L Bendixen, a pilot/physician and Flight Surgeon of the 185th, had landed his A-7 just minutes prior to the crash. An ambulance from the 185th TAC Clinic picked him up and took the colonel to the crash site. Col. Bendixen was the first doctor on the scene. Another guardsmen at the scene was Staff Sergeant Lynn Harter. Sergeant Harter removed a three year old boy out of his seat in the wrecked shell of the aircraft's cabin and gave him to Lt. Col. Dennis Nielsen, the Group's safety officer.

The young child was Spencer Bailey. A statue memorializing this event stands in Sioux City's riverfront development, located near the Anderson Dance Pavilion.

Between the day of the tragedy and days after, Air Guardsmen, equipment, and facilities contributed largely to the effort. Relief agencies set up command posts and offices on base. United Airlines, the Red Cross, and the Salvation Army were there. The Weapons Load Trailer was used for the morgue command post. Offices and phones were set up for the survivors to use. Barracks and dining hall were used by all volunteers to get some rest, food, and drink.

The 185th, as with all of Siouxland, showed their Midwest attitude of hospitality and kindness. So many doctors, nurses, and EMTs showed up at the hospitals that they had an overabundance. Neighbors and strangers would take the dirty clothes and wash them. A call for blood was not needed, as over 400 showed up at the blood bank. And the local communities around Sioux City all pitched in.

1990 started with another Snowbird expedition to Davis-Monthan AFB, Arizona, starting January 20th. Thirteen A-7s, with the support of 134 personnel, went west to escape the Sioux City winter, but surprise, it snowed in Tucson. During those two weeks they flew 184 sorties. No sooner did the Tucson troops return home than three A-7s, four pilots, and twelve maintenance personnel were

July 19, 1989, was a day that all of Sioux City will remember. That was the day that a United Airlines DC-10, Flight 232, crashed at Sioux Gateway Airport. The cornfields gave some safety in this horrible tragedy. The location where the DC-10 first touched down is now part of the property occupied by the Mid America Museum of Aviation and Transportation. (*185th TFG/McCallum collection*)

Big and little parts of the DC-10 were scattered over a large area. (*185th TFG/McCallum collection*)

on the road for McChord AFB, Washington state, for 14 days supporting the Army. Two more A-7s were needed, with maintenance support, to aid the 132nd Fighter Wing in an Operational Readiness Inspection that they were going through at Volk Field, Wisconsin.

International travel was awaiting. Once again they were traveling to St. Truiden AB, Belgium. There they participated in exercise Coronet Canyon between May 28th and June 27th. This was a combined Checkered Flag/NATO exercise, in which they were involved in joint air/ground operations. This type of exercise prepared U.S. and NATO military for possible Soviet aggression and was a direct show of power for the Soviets and their allies.

For the Group's outstanding effort in the United Flight 232 crash and cleanup afterwards, their

Flight surgeon Col. (Dr.) Romaine L. Bendixen had just landed his A-7 and was in position to render aid shortly after the accident. (*185th TFG/McCallum collection*)

participation in the defense of the Panama Canal, Gunsmoke 89, and other deployments, they were notified July 1, 1990, that they were selected as the outstanding Air National Guard unit and were the recipient of the Spaatz Trophy once again.

On August 2nd, Iraqi forces invaded Kuwait. Though reserve forces were not called up initially, a number of 185th personnel from its fire department volunteered. They were used to fill vacancies at U.S. bases where personnel had been sent overseas. The 174th and it's A-7s were not called upon.

Though not called upon for the Iraq/Kuwait conflict, they remained ready. In October, six A-7s supported by 78 personnel went to Eglin AFB, Florida. There they participated in Air-Ground Operations School/Combat Hammer 91. They worked with Army and Air Force Forward Air Controllers. They also had the experience of firing live Hughes AGM-65 Maverick air-to-ground missiles at ground targets.

1991 saw the 174th Tactical Fighter Squadron start the process of transitioning from the A-7D to the General Dynamics F-16C Fighting Falcon.

The 174th became world-wide travelers with their A-7s. They traveled to Belgium a number of times, as shown on this 1990 deployment. (*185th TFG/McCallum collection*)

They continued the usual: Snowbird in January/February, where they got to handle live ordnance under simulated combat conditions; to Buckley ANG Base in Colorado in March for Turkey Shoot, the ANG A-7 gunnery competition; Red Flag at Nellis AFB, Nevada, in June, where they performed ground attack missions, aerial combat, and employed electronic countermeasures; and summer encampment at Volk Field, Wisconsin, in August.

But more and more of their time was in preparation for the F-16. The last five A-7Ds flew out of Sioux City February 20, 1991, for the bone yard at Tucson. There were a few left, but they were intended to become static displays on base and in surrounding communities.

A-7D in flight. (*185th TFG/McCallum collection*)

Loading AGKM-65 Maverick air-to-ground missiles for some range practice. (*185th TFG/McCallum collection*)

The final color scheme of the 174th A-7. (*185th TFG/McCallum collection*)

Chapter Eleven

The Bats Go High Tech

Whether they realized it or not, at the beginning of 1991, the next two years were going to be a time of transition. Speculation was rampant for quite a while that the 174th Tactical Fighter Squadron would be trading in their A-7Ds for the F-16C. From their latest Air Force gunnery competitions, the crews said that the F-16 made the A-7 "look like a dump truck." The National Guard Bureau advised Col. Dennis B. Swanstrom, 185th Tactical Fighter Group commander, that the 185th would be starting conversion to the F-16 soon.

The initial phase of the changeover was the arrival of a Site Activation Task Force. This Task Force arrived at the Sioux City ANG Base March 4, 1991, to determine if the base could handle the F-16, and what actions would be necessary for a smooth transition to the new aircraft. Much would be needed to accommodate the new aircraft and all its new systems.

A lot was happening in the first half of the 1990s. They received their first two F-16Cs December 19, 1991; the squadron and group were redesignated Fighter (from Tactical Fighter) March 16, 1992; and the Sioux City Air Guard went to Wing strength (185th Fighter Wing) October 1, 1995. (*185th TFG/McCallum collection*)

Modified and expanded existing facilities and the construction of new facilities were needed. Planning and obtaining funds for the expansion proceeded throughout all of 1991. With the new aircraft and mission, an electronic countermeasures facility had to be added to the existing Avionics/Weapons Release building. The ramp area behind the ANG hangar needed to be replaced in order to handle the added weight of an F-16. Remodeling of the Fuel Cell/Corrosion Control facility and the Operations Building was needed. New construction included a Munitions Maintenance/Storage complex and Civil Engineering complex. The cost of all this would be over 20 million dollars.

Training was a Group-wide effort. Pilots had to learn the new aircraft and all of its systems. The maintenance people, from the flight line crews to all the shop personnel, had to learn the basic aircraft (airframe and engine), as well as all the complicated electronic systems. Then there was the supply system, technical orders, and the administrative functions so necessary to keeping the Group running smoothly.

The first two F-16Cs arrived at Sioux City ANG Base December 19, 1991. Additional F-16Cs and a two-place F-16D would be received in 1992. In 1991, the 40 pilots that would fly the F-16 attended ground school when they were not flying the A-7. As the last flying A-7s left Sioux City February 20, 1992, the pilots were fully emerged in transition training. Throughout 1992, groups of the 174th pilots attended three-month transition courses at either

Aerial view of Sioux Gateway Airport in the 1990s. Still visible are the cross runways of the original early-1940s airport shown left of center at the top of the photo. (*185th TFG/McCallum collection*)

McConnell AFB, Kansas; Luke AFB, Arizona; or MacDill AFB, Florida. At these bases they learned to fly the F-16 expertly and learned their many systems. An additional 45-day training period back at Sioux City followed, where they worked with an instructor pilot prior to being certified in the F-16.

At the same time, the maintenance personnel were learning their trade in the F-16. Maintenance personnel attended Air Force schools as funds allowed. By September 1991, twenty maintenance personnel from the Consolidated Aircraft Maintenance Squadron went to MacDill AFB, Florida, and McConnell AFB, Kansas, for formal training. As time and funds allowed others followed, going to a number of Air Force bases. Starting in January 1992, 14 instructors from the 527th Field Training Detachment came to Sioux City to carry on maintenance training for four months.

With the new aircraft and expanded mission that they brought, additional personnel were needed. About 100 more were required. Adding to this need was the fact that around 100 personnel whose enlistment would be up in 1992 were not expected to reenlist. The recruiting staff of the 185th put on a great effort to recruit new troops from the surrounding area. Their effort included setting up a booth at the local mall, which proved to be quite productive.

Lots was going on during this two year period. In June 1991, the 185th was awarded their fourth Air Force Outstanding Unit award. In late October, the Site Activation Task Force returned to perform a follow-up survey to determine how preparations were going. The good news was that they received a Satisfactory rating and all progressed ahead.

In September, the Air Force announced a massive restructuring. Among the changes, Tactical Air Command and Strategic Air Command were being inactivated, and taking their place was a new Air Combat Command. Included in the changes was that the Air Force was eliminating the designation

The callsign of the 174th while serving in Vietnam was Bat. Thus, they became known as the Bats. While flying the F-16, the Bat symbol was at its zenith. Here the Bat caricature has been added to a wall in the hangar. (*185th TFG/McCallum collection*)

A very aggressive version of the Bat was adopted for the outer surfaces of the F-16's two vertical stabilizers. (*185th TFG/McCallum collection*)

"Tactical" from their unit designations. On March 16, 1992, the 185th Tactical Fighter Group became the 185th Fighter Group, and the 174th Tactical Fighter Squadron became the 174th Fighter Squadron.

The new aircraft got a uniquely 174th Fighter Squadron motif—a bat. Staff Sgt. Frank Rosales, a graphic specialist in the 185th, came up with an attacking bat emblem that takes up a good portion of the outer surfaces of the F-16's vertical stabilizer. All of the squadron's F-16s would carry this proud symbol.

Initial operations with the F-16 started in April 1992. On the 15th they were rated operational. The next day, Lt. Col. Norm Frank and Lt. Col. Les Jensen inaugurated flight operations. The F-16s with the Sioux City Guard spent about an hour "punching holes in the sky," as the 185th's 50th Year History book states. The rest of the year was spent qualifying the squadron pilots in the F-16 and training the maintenance personnel in its care and feeding. They would continue to receive additional F-16Cs and one two-place F-16D well into 1992.

On February 6, 1993, the 174th got to show what they had learned. On that date they left Sioux City for one of their two-week Snowbird exercises at Davis-Monthan AFB, Arizona. It was a busy time, dropping bombs and shooting at targets. Simulated air-to-air combat was conducted against Marine Corps F/A-18s and Air Force F-15Es. During their stay in Arizona they flew 157 sorties, which included time working with Army Forward Air Controllers.

In May, the pilots and maintenance crew received more practice honing their F-16 skills. First they went to Gulfport, Mississippi, to participate in Dissimilar Air Combat Training/Air Combat Maneuvering training. At about the same time, another group of F-16s and support personnel went to Nellis AFB, Nevada. Here they participated in Air Combat Command's Longshot exercise. Longshot replaced a number of former Tactical Air Command and Strategic Air Command competitions. Some 250 aircraft from Air Combat Command, Air Force Reserve, and Air National Guard participated. A-10s, B-1Bs, B-52Hs, F-15s, and F-16s formed teams in what was a bombing competition and bomber/fighter integration to accomplish a bombing mission. In these missions, pitched battles were waged against aggressor forces of U.S. Navy A-4s, F-14s, and F/A-18s. The 174th scored seven aerial kills against the aggressors.

What would be called the Persian Gulf War, aka Operation Desert Storm, began August 2, 1990. This would be the beginning of decades of tensions and combat. As the 174th Tactical Fighter Squadron had A-7Ds, the unit was not called upon to support the combat effort. Since the 174th Fighter Squadron was equipped with the modern F-16C in 1993, they were. The Kurdish uprising in 1991 and Saddam Hussein's retaliation brought about a United Nations resolution that authorized Operation Provide Comfort on April 5, 1991. Operation Provide Comfort II began July 24th, in which allied airpower protected the Kurds with a no-fly zone in northern Iraq.

During the summer of 1993, the 185th Fighter Group and three other Air Guard groups were notified that they would provide aircraft and support personnel as part of Provide Comfort II. Besides the 185th, the 114th from Sioux Falls, South Dakota; 140th from Denver, Colorado; and the 192nd from

The tails of this F-16C display the Bat symbol for all to see. At the base of the verticals the chieftain's head, a symbol of the 174th for decades, is incorporated into the state markings. Also, the Air Force Outstanding Unit ribbons can be seen on the nose of the squadron's aircraft. (*185th TFG/McCallum collection*)

A 1990s view of the ANG base at Sioux Gateway Airport. With each change in aircraft, buildings were modified and new buildings added. (*185th TFG/McCallum collection*)

Hangar maintenance looks somewhat like a child's toy being taken apart. Note in the background the Bat painted on the hangar floor. (*185th TFG/McCallum collection*)

Hangar full of F-16s. (*185th TFG/McCallum collection*)

Richmond, Virginia, were called up. They would be operating out of Incirlik AB, Turkey, where they would spend 45 days on each tour of duty. On November 29th, three of the 174th Fighter Squadron's F-16s and a C-130 with 40 support personnel left Sioux City for the Middle East. Their mission was to identify and intercept any Iraqi Air Force fighters north of the 36th parallel. During their 45 days, each of the pilots flew 14 missions. Though on a couple of occasions Iraqi Air Force aircraft were picked up at a distance, there was no encounter with them during the 174th's flights. The Kurd's guardians from Sioux City returned home January 16, 1994.

A pair of F-16s roar off the runway to protect the skies. Their protection was felt by U.S. President George W. Bush September 11, 2001. (*185th TFG/McCallum collection*)

Provide Comfort II continued in 1995 for a number of Air Guard units. The 174th Fighter Squadron sent four F-16s, supported by about 180 maintenance personnel from the 185th Consolidated Aircraft Maintenance Squadron, to Incirlik AB again on March 6th. At Incirlik, the 174th operated with the 199th Fighter Squadron of the Hawaiian Air National Guard. One joint operation that they participated in concerned the availability of food for their troops. Because Incirlik was a large base obtaining food was quite a task, they jointly set up a coffee shop named Bat Cafe, serving breakfast and lunch in the flight line area.

The missions were quite long for the pilots. It took about 45 minutes to go to their assigned areas in northern Iraq from Turkey. There they would get fuel from a tanker and patrol from one and a half hours to over three hours. While on patrol, the fighter pilots worked with Airborne Warning and Control (AWACs) aircraft. During their 35-day tour the aircrews flew more than 200 sorties, accumulating almost 730 flight hours. Like the unit personnel that were deployed to Vietnam during 1968 and 1969, the personnel in Turkey in 1995 looked into performing the same human kindness. They found that there was an organization on base called Project Orphanage that helped orphanages in the surrounding area. The 185th personnel gladly joined in the effort.

While some of the personnel partook in Provide Comfort II, those back at Sioux City were flying other missions. Such exercises as Snowbird in the warm west, Maple Leaf at Cold Lake, Canada, and air combat training at Gulfport, Mississippi, were included in their activities. A trip to Karup Air Station, Denmark, included the Sioux City troops in another NATO exercise. Then there were the Operational Readiness Exercises, Operational Readiness Inspections, and mobilization practices. In 1995, they had an Operational Readiness Inspection at Volk Field, Wisconsin. They were ready, as they had a practice Operational Readiness Inspection back at the base the month before. Now that the IG inspectors were watching and grading them the pressure was on. They were simulating being at a forward operating base in Europe. The scenario was that it was wartime, and they were receiving SCUD missile and chemical attacks. They passed and were declared combat ready.

The 174th pilots learned air refueling in their F-100C days and remained experts ever since. Also, with the air refueling capability the squadron has served all over the world. (*185th TFG/McCallum collection*)

One of the squadron's two F-16D two-place aircraft. (*185th TFG/McCallum collection*)

In late 1995, once again, the Air National Guard had to change its structure to match the present one in the U.S. Air Force. On October 1, 1995, the 185th Fighter Wing was activated at Sioux City ANG Base with Col. Dennis B. Swanstrom, who had commanded the Group, now as wing commander.

Back to Incirlik AB, Turkey. In the summer of 1996, the 185th Fighter Wing sent personnel to patrol the Iraq northern no-fly zone. This effort made news back home. On July 10, 1996, in both the House and Senate of Iowa, a "concurrent resolution supporting the 185th Fighter Wing of the Air National Guard of Iowa in its peacekeeping patrols in the United Nations 'No-Fly Zone' over Iraq" was entered.

May 1996 marked a point of history for the Sioux City Air Guard. It was then that they had their first female pilot, 2nd Lt. Bobbi J. Doorenbos. It took time for some fellow pilots to accept the fact that a female was capable of flying the F-16, or should. Eventually she would participate in such deployments as Operation Southern Watch and Operation Iraqi Freedom.

1996 also marked the 50th anniversary of the 174th. As part of the celebration, the Wing's commander, Col. Dennis B. Swanstrom, had the Wing paint one of the F-16s gold for their golden anniversary. Col. Swanstrom stated that in the case of an emergency the plane could be returned to the standard color scheme within 24 hours.

Operation Southern Watch started in August 1992, to ensure Iraqi compliance with United Nations Resolution 688. As a result of the resolution, a no-fly zone was established from the 32nd Parallel, which was changed to the 33rd Parallel in 1996. A number of Air National Guard units participated with joint international forces in patrolling the area. In late 1995, the 185th was informed that they would be joining the patrolling force in 1996. In January 1996, Lt. Col. John P. Janson visited Al-Jabar AB, Kuwait, to survey what the 185th would be coming in to. A total of 10 pilots and 83 Guardsmen would serve during this deployment, but not for the full stay. They would be rotating, and only 30 would be there at a time. With those rotating to Kuwait, a total of about 140 took part in the operation. All members deployed were volunteers.

The F-16 and the supporting members left on March 12th, led by Lt. Col. Janson, the detachment commander. All but the pilots flew by commercial airliner. There was very little equipment for the 185th to take, as the Air Guard unit they were relieving (175th Fighter Squadron/114th Fighter Wing) was leaving their equipment for the Iowans. During their five weeks of operations from Kuwait, the pilots would fly six to eight sorties per day.

There was one new modern convenience for the folks back home. The families could video teleconference with their loved ones. Equipment was set up in the Sioux City ANG Base guard shack, where the families could stop by any time, 24 hours a day, and use it.

The 174th Fighter Squadron sent six F-16s to the Caribbean, where they operated out of the island

In May 1996, 2nd Lt. Bobbi Jo Doorenbos graduated from flight school and became the 174th's first female pilot. She is shown with her father, Rodney Jay Doorenbos, in this 1997 photo. Rodney Doorenbos flew with the 174th in the F-100 days. (*McCallum photo*)

In the summer of 1995, the Collins Foundation B-17G Nine-O-Nine had its landing gear collapse while landing at Sioux Gateway Airport. The ANG fire department attended to the accident, and fortunately, the aircraft was repairable. Also, a 174th retiree came to the rescue. Bob Stolze had been a B-17 maintenance instructor during World War II, and at the time of the B-17 incident he was working as an aircraft mechanic at the airport. With Bob's help, the Collins Foundation was able to fly the B-17 out of Sioux Gateway. (*185th TFG/McCallum collection*)

In 1996, the 174th/185th celebrated its 50th anniversary—it's Golden Anniversary. In celebration of this occasion, 185th Fighter Wing commander Col. Dennis B. Swanstrom had his paint shop paint F-16C 85-565 gold. (*185th TFG/McCallum collection*)

of Curacao. Under the command of Lt. Col. Gary Cranmer, they searched for suspicious aircraft flying out of Columbia and Venezuela. A support team of about 200 went along for the seven-week deployment in the summer of 2000.

The biggest announcement, or maybe shock, of 2000, was that after 53 years of flying single-engine fighter type aircraft, they were scheduled to transition into Boeing KC-135 tankers.

The 185th was shocked when Col. V. Tomas "T.C." Considine passed away from a lengthy illness. Col. John P. Janson was appointed acting Wing commander immediately; he was officially appointed commander October 13th.

In preparation for their forthcoming transition to tankers, Col. Janson and his staff were attending their first conference with Air Mobility Command in Washington, D.C., on September 11, 2001.

North American Aerospace Defense Command (NORAD), like all of America, was trying to figure out what was going on. In mid-morning, NORAD contacted the 185th and inquired as to their capability to launch aircraft. Within minutes the first group of F-16s was in the air. Not long after a second group took to the skies, this time with ammunition. Around noon, a third group was airborne with guns loaded and air-to-air missiles.

All civilian traffic had been grounded by this time, and only military aircraft were supposedly in the air, except for the lady in her new aircraft, who had somehow shut off her radio. Apparently she was surprised to find two F-16s on her wings. After she hurriedly turned on her radio she obeyed the fighters' orders to land, as they escorted her to an airfield at O'Neill, Nebraska. The third group airborne was instructed to go to Offutt AFB, Nebraska, and fly a Combat Air Patrol over the base. About an hour into their patrol they detected a large plane approaching from the southeast. They locked on to the approaching plane, but immediately were ordered from ground control not to lock on the plane; it was Air Force One. The President's plane landed, and after a while took off without any sign of its escort. The Sioux City fighters, who had recently received fuel from a tanker, were informed that they were to escort Air Force One! From there they escorted the President to the vicinity of Andrews AFB, Maryland, where the escort duty was taken over by local fighters. The two pilots for the Bats were Kurt Kindschuh and Tyson Herbold.

As the story goes, it was a great recruiting tool and brought attention to the 185th. But higher headquarters did not see it in such a favorable light. Though Swanstrom told them the aircraft could be repainted within 24 hours, they put pressure on the colonel to repaint it in standard scheme. He did. However, the higher ups must have had a change of heart, because they requested the gold F-16 for an event. Too late—it had been repainted. (*185th TFG/McCallum collection*)

A 174th F-16C takes off from Sioux Gateway Airport on an air-intercept training mission. (*185th TFG/McCallum collection*)

Preparing for some flying over a bombing range, armorers bring a trailer loaded with bombs to the flight line to load on F-16s. (*185th TFG/McCallum collection*)

A F-16 of the 174th on patrol in the skies over the upper Midwest. (*185th TFG/McCallum collection*)

With the command staff in Washington, D.C., and not able to get out, it was up to the personnel back at Sioux City to run the show. The outcome showed that they were a well-trained, capable, efficient organization. One of the people stepping up to the job was then-Major Brian Miller who, today as a colonel, is the Wing commander. Also assisting with the fast and furious actions and communications that morning was Arthur Kirchgasler.

September 11th brought about the concept of Homeland Defense and a number of programs, including a new federal department. One of these homeland defense operations was Noble Eagle. Noble Eagle involved Army and Air Force units, and evolved into an international effort. Early on, U.S. fighters flew combat air patrol over the cities of Washington, D.C. and New York. The 174th Fighter Squadron performed some of the flights over New York City.

In spite of the terrorist actions of the past September, the whole of Sioux City Air Guard carried on. They went to Prince Sultan AB, Kingdom of Saudi Arabia, in October. Six F-16s, with six additional pilots and 60 support personnel, were once again enforcing Operation Southern Watch. This would be the last overseas deployment in the F-16.

For the diehard fighter pilots, 2002 and into 2003 was a road to the end. In 2002, there was a lot of planning and preparation going on, including construction. The final day of operations for the F-16 came on December 20th. It was not long before the last F-16 left the base on January 16, 2003. It was the end of one story and a bitter pill for some. But the 185th Wing, with its flying squadron, the 174th, would once again show what they were made of. As the 185th Air Refueling Wing, many more vital missions would be flown and awards garnered.

The crew chief is checking things out in this F-16 as the ordnance troops prepare to upload tons of destruction. (*185th TFG/McCallum collection*)

Chapter Twelve

Gas Station in the Sky

2002 was a year of early transition. It would see the last operations with the F-16 and the beginnings of transition into the tanker game.

The 174th Tactical Fighter Squadron, with a support team from the 185th, left for an exercise called Air Warrior. Six F-16s and about 100 support personnel left Sioux City April 13th. This would be a joint Army and Air Force exercise taking place near the Army National Training Center at Fort Irwin, California. The fighters staged out of Nellis AFB, Nevada, which was east across the mountain range from Fort Irwin.

They operated in a large area; Army National Training Center covers over 1,000 square miles of desert and mountains. The scenario for the exercise was two forces of 5,000 to 6,000 each battling in an Afghanistan-like environment. The 174th pilots were providing air-to-ground support, working with ground Forward Air Controllers. Compared to the F-100Cs the 174th flew in Vietnam, where they worked with Forward Air Controllers, this exercise in California was quite high tech. Here the Forward Air Controllers sent enemy location information to the F-16s via data link using a system called Situation Awareness Data Link. The information was displayed on the F-16's Tactical Air Display. The F-16s then went for the target. The F-16 pilot would either use his own precision attack targeting system, called Lightning II, or have Army troops on the ground light up the target with their laser equipment.

A high point of 2002 for all of Sioux City occurred May 25th, when Sioux Gateway Airport, which includes the ANG Base, was renamed Sioux Gateway Airport/Col. Bud Day Field in honor of Col. George E. "Bud" Day, a Sioux City native and war hero who was awarded the Medal of Honor. Colonel Day passed away July 27, 2013.

The 174th's last deployment was in October, when they went to Portland, Oregon, for Dissimilar Air Combat training with the 123rd Fighter Squadron, which flew F-15s. Here they practiced aerial combat with the F-15s at 30,000 feet over the Pacific Ocean. This was a time of mixed feelings for these pilots of the 174th. During the day they had to give their full attention to their F-16s and what they were doing. At night other thoughts crept into their minds. 9/11 was just a year ago. Also, for the first time the squadron would no longer be flying a single-seat, single-engine fighter-type aircraft. They were going to be flying a quite large, four-engine, airliner-size aircraft. This conversion was going to be quite complex, compared to all the others the squadron had gone through in its past.

That sad day arrived. The 174th Fighter Squadron flew their last mission in the F-16C December 20, 2002. Lt. Col. Jim Walker led the flight of five on a training mission. Soon after, the 18 F-16s in the 174th's stable would be leaving Sioux City for good. They were all destined for the 138th Fighter Squadron at Hancock Field, Syracuse, of the New York ANG.

The end came on January 16, 2003, when the last five F-16s left Sioux City for Syracuse, New York. Leading this flight as he did on the squadron's last sortie in December, Lt. Col. Jim Walker had many emotions about what was to come, as did most of the

When the 174th Fighter Squadron pilots flying F-16Cs received fuel from a KC-135 on many of their missions, there was no thought that someday the roles would be switched. When it happened it hit the unit hard. As it turned out, it probably prolonged the longevity of the squadron as a flying unit. (*185th TFG/McCallum collection*)

unit. Also on this flight was Major Chuck Taylor, who was on that last mission in December. This was not just the fighters departing, it was a change of mission ceremony. It included a short speech by Wing commander Col. John P. Janson as the F-16s taxied by the Guard hangar, where the Guard personnel and civilian spectators watched, already painted with the logo of the New York unit. For those present a short video was shown about the KC-135E.

This was a change of aircraft ceremony. About 10 minutes after the last F-16s departed, a KC-135E of the 116th Air Refueling Squadron, 141st Air Refueling Wing from Spokane, Washington, landed and pulled up to the 185th's hangar for all to inspect. As all of the KC-135Es that the 174th would receive would be from the 116th, this was more than fitting. The 174th would eventually get this same aircraft later. With their new aircraft and mission, the Sioux City Guard had a new member added to their flight crews—the refueling boom operator. Master Sergeant David Dietrich, who was one of the early "boomers" that had completed the four-month boom operator course December 20, 2002, was to go aboard the visiting KC-135 and talk with its boom operator, Master Sergeant Sheri Paplham. Sergeant

The tail flash of the 174th Air Refueling Squadron, 185th Air Refueling Wing's KC-135s continues the Bat legacy. (*185th ARW*)

Dietrich was not the only 174th crew member to be trained in the KC-135. 2nd Lt. Brian Thompson had entered the one-year Air Force flight training, thinking he was going to be a F-16 pilot in the 174th Fighter Squadron. While still in training, the change in mission was announced and he ended up going into six months of tanker training, and was qualified as a co-pilot in the KC-135 just prior to the January 16th ceremony.

It was for the preservation of the 185th that the change took hold. Then, as in 2012, change in Air Force needs and missions impacted the Air Guard. Iowa Air National Guard headquarters saw the writing on the wall. Then-current Air Force needs did not include two fighter squadrons in that state, but tanker needs were ever-increasing, with all that was going on in the Middle East. This trend started with the 1991 Gulf War and has continued. In 2000, Iowa's Adjutant General, Major General Ron Dardis, and Deputy Adjutant General, Brig. Gen. Joseph E. Lucas, with state support approached the U.S. Air Force for an alternative mission as a tanker unit. As reported in the *Sioux City Journal* on January 16, 2003, they "aggressively went for it." They found favor with the Air Force, and in September 2000 announced that the 185th Fighter Wing would change to a KC-135 tanker outfit. This would be a costly change. For construction (modifying existing structures and building new ones), training, and equipment, it was estimated about $60 million would be required.

Another standard emblem on the unit's KC-135s is the outline of the state of Iowa, with the location of Sioux City indicated and usually the words "Pride of Siouxland." (*185th ARW*)

Training started in 2002 while they were still flying F-16 missions. Early training was indoctrination classes on base. The 141st Air Refueling Wing at Spokane, Washington, assisted in maintenance training. Not only was this aircraft bigger, but it was not as modern as the F-16s in built-in diagnostics. From the engines to the avionics it was more work. At the same time, there was less repair work that could be accomplished on base and more that had to be sent to depot level facilities at other bases. By the time the last F-16 left Sioux City, 20 maintenance troops had been trained and would serve as instructors for the remaining maintenance personnel, as well as having the responsibility of checking out the tankers coming to Sioux City before they left Spokane and after they arrived in Iowa. There was a long way to go, as the 185th had approximately 500 more to train.

Boom operator training started in 2002. The training was a four-month course given by the 54th Air Refueling Squadron at Altus AFB, Oklahoma. To practice their trade after the Altus training, the boom operators flew with the other Air Guard units. The squadron estimated that 20 boom operators would be required when they had their full complement of KC-135s.

The 174th would need 45 pilots when they had their full complement of KC-135s. In 2002, two new pilots that completed flight school went to Altus AFB, like the "boomers," for KC-135 flight training. But as a number of Air Guard units were converting to tankers, Altus was soon over-booked. Because of that, the USAF developed a transition course at McConnell AFB, Wichita, Kansas. Because most of the pilots in 2002 did not need initial pilot training, the conversion course at McConnell satisfied the requirements. The only problem was that McConnell did not have a KC-135E simulator, as the Air Force was flying the upgraded R-model. The solution was that Scott AFB, Illinois, still had an E Simulator. The Sioux City pilots then took their academics and flew the simulator at Scott, then went to McConnell for flights in the real thing. A pilot needed about 60

KC-135E in flight. It would take over a year to transition into the tankers and to become operationally ready. (*185th ARW*)

hours of flight time in the KC-135 to be qualified. Besides the two pilots fresh from pilot training, there were 10 squadron pilots that were in the pipeline for retraining in the KC-135E. Major Brian Miller, future commander of the Wing, was the first 185th F-16 pilot to complete transition flight training.

That Saturday, January 18th, 2003, a Farewell to the Fighter program was held. This event included a briefing on the tanker conversion program at the ANG base, followed by a pilots-only, past and present, event at a local hotel. As has been the custom of pilots from the early age of military flying, they gathered at the local watering hole for comfort and camaraderie. In this instance, it was Eddie's Lounge in nearby Sergeant Bluff. Eddie's was a local institution in which the Air Guard pilots, and others, had been gathering for 45 years. The lounge enjoyed international attention. On one of the squadron's trips to Incirlik, Turkey, a sign exclaimed "Eddie's West 6100 miles."

In March, construction was underway. Their current hangar was being enlarged and ramp space was being increased. Because of all the fuel the KC-135 needs, a hydrant system for fuelling had to be installed. Other buildings were being modified for change of purpose. On the aircraft maintenance side, over 40 more personnel went to Fairchild AFB for additional training.

At this point, the entire 185th Fighter Wing was going through phases of emotions. There was the anger over what was happening. Then the denial phase. Most arrived at the point where they accepted that life would go on and accepted what was happening. Some had a harder time with the change. Four of the 30 pilots chose to go to other fighter squadrons before the last five F-16s had left the base, and four more would choose to leave before the end of summer.

The first KC-135E arrived April 23rd from the 116th Air Refueling Squadron at Fairchild AFB, Spokane, Washington. The community was not invited to this event due to security, but the news media, as well as Wing personnel, were on hand to welcome the aircraft. It had been three months since any operational aircraft had been parked on the Air Guard ramp. This one would see very little flying for some time, as it was intended to serve as hands-on training for the maintenance personnel. The Washington Air Guard had already applied Sioux City markings on the tanker.

A second KC-135 arrived around the end of April. Like the first, it was destined for maintenance training. A great asset to the 174th in its transition was Captain Adam McLean, who joined the squadron after accumulating some 2,500 hours flying the KC-

135 in the USAF. While construction continued throughout the spring and summer of 2003, the pilots that had completed the conversion, along with the trained boom operators, flew with other Air National Guard refueling squadrons to maintain their expertise.

On June 1, 2003, the 185th Wing and 174th Squadron were redesignated Air Refueling. By late summer, a third KC-135E was at Sioux City. It, and one of the earlier aircraft that initially was for maintenance training, were being flown. They also had two more KC-135Es at McConnell AFB, Kansas, being used in the flight training there. The first takeoff and landing with an all-185th crew occurred October 21st. Major Miller was the pilot on this flight, which was a local sortie. As construction would continue into 2004, more funding was in the process of going through Congress. At the airport, Phase I of taxiway work was completed in early October. This was required due to the heavy weight of the KC-135. The following month, the new Fuel Cell/Corrosion Control hangar was completed, a $7.7 million project. This hangar allowed the maintenance personnel to work on the complex fuel transfer system of the KC-135 in a protected environment.

A big step forward was accomplished when the underground fuel and hydrant system was completed and operational. Six hydrants were installed in the Guard's ramp area. Prior to this, it was not a problem to fill an F-16 with 1,000 gallons of fuel from a truck. But filling a KC-135E with 30,000 gallons was quite a different matter. This system did a lot: fuel storage, distribution, and when needed, fuel could be taken from a plane if maintenance was required. Fuel testing was also accomplished to insure the quality of the fuel.

The number of KC-135Es the 174th Air Refueling Squadron would be flying remained in flux as April 2004 opened. On the 7th, one of their tankers, along with an additional crew, left Sioux City for Forbes AFB, Topeka, Kansas, to get the squadron's ninth and supposedly last aircraft. Originally they thought they would get ten, but it had been reduced by one. Within about a year they would receive a tenth aircraft. This was a dual mission flight. Both on their way to Kansas and the return trip, the crew would refuel other aircraft.

Up to this point, the aircrews were flying two classes of training missions: local and long distance. The local flights usually consisted of refueling F-16s out of Sioux Falls, South Dakota, or Des Moines, Iowa. These flights lasted 2.7 hours to 4 hours. In April 2004, these local flights accounted for

The Patriot and The Veteran were colorful memorials painted on two of the squadron's KC-135Es. (*185th ARW*)

about 60 percent of their missions. Missions were flown around the U.S. to give the boom operators experience in refueling different kinds of aircraft. Missions to Whiteman AFB, Missouri, were flown to refuel B-1s; Offutt AFB, Omaha, Nebraska, to refuel RC-135s; and Tinker AFB, Oklahoma City, Oklahoma, to refuel E-3 AWACS. They also flew across the oceans in support of fighter squadrons deploying overseas. In these missions they could also support fighter squadron maintenance personnel. Through August 2004, the 174th had flown to Alaska, Britain, Germany, Iceland, and Hawaii on these support missions.

Cope Thunder 04-02 was the 174th's first exercise as an air refueling squadron. This Alaskan exercise was conducted between August 11th and the 27th. Both of Alaska's Air Force Bases (Eielson and Elmendorf) were staging areas for USAF, Air National Guard, and Air Force Reserve, as well as Naval aircraft. For this operation, the 185th/174th sent two KC-135s and 57 personnel.

This exercise has been described as "the largest multilateral air combat exercise in the Pacific." Its objective was to prepare air expeditionary forces for deployments and to ready the Navy counterparts for carrier deployments. Some 1,300 personnel participated in the exercise. F-15s, F-16s, and F/A18s provided fighter support, while electronics/surveillance were done by EA-6B, E-2C, and E-3B. KC-135s from Sioux City, McConnell AFB, Kansas, and Bangor, Maine, provided aerial refueling. The 174th Air Refueling Squadron flew 11 sorties totaling 48 flight hours. During these flights, 62 hook-ups to other aircraft were accomplished and 261,200 pounds of fuel were provided.

In September, the unit deployed to the NATO air base at Geilenkirchen, Germany. There they provided air refueling support for NATO E-3 AWACS aircraft. Deployments like this would become the usual from about this point on. They would send one KC-135 with two crews (pilot, copilot, and boom operator), plus three crew chiefs to support the flying. They would deploy to a foreign base, where they would remain for about a week and fly every day.

One of the KC-135Es going on a training mission. (*185th ARW*)

By mid-May 2005, the 174th Air Refueling Squadron was up to its full strength of 10 KC-135Es. They had a busy flying schedule, with four to six training sorties each day, seven days a week. When they were a fighter wing, they operated four days a week, ten hours a day. Now it was all hours of the day, seven days a week. At this time they had flown their KC-135s to 13 countries, including support for Afghanistan operations. Though they had started with 22 of the pilots remaining from the fighter days and recruiting others, they were in need of four more pilots at this time.

In 2005, the History Channel was airing a very popular program called "Mail Call." Hosting the program was a unique personality, retired Marine Gunnery Sergeant R. Lee Ermey. Ermey's intent was to educate the public about the military—past, present, and future. Questions submitted by viewers were explained within the time confines of the program on any military subject.

On May 13, 2005, the 174th Air Refueling Squadron was scheduled to fly south and refuel one of the 509th Bomb Wing's B-2s out of Whiteman AFB, Missouri. But to their surprise, they received a call from Whiteman prior to takeoff, informing them that because of the timing of their refueling, they would be videotaped for a segment of "Mail Call" on the B-2 Stealth Bomber.

Flying the KC-135 was Major Sean Masin, an instructor pilot, and Captain Tyson Herbold as copilot. They arrived on station, but the History Channel crew was still filming Whiteman. Time kept being rescheduled until the film crew was ready. They finally showed up. Not only was there the B-2, but an accompanying T-33 with a cameraman that flew all over to get various shots of the action. Back in the business end of the KC-135 were boom operators Chief Master Sergeant Tony Fortney and Master Sergeant James Hill. As they hooked up to the bomber and provided some 4,500 gallons of fuel, they could see Ermey in the copilot's seat filming them. Within the tanker, 185th multimedia manager Master Sergeant Vince De Groot was also filming the operation, which was given to History Channel afterwards.

At the conclusion of the refueling Ermey did as was his habit at the end of each program, "Semper Fi—Hoo Rah!" The B-2 segment was aired June 10th, 2005.

2005 was a very uncertain time for military installations and units. A Defense Base Closure and Realignment Commission, better known as BRAC, was looking very hard at National Guard, Reserve, and active military of all branches. With their willing switch to tankers, the 185th Air Refueling Wing felt fairly safe, though they knew that they, too, were a possible candidate. Prior to accepting

Hoo-Rah! to Sergeant R. Lee Ermey. Part the 174th ARS participation in History Channel's "Mail Call" included refueling a B-2 from Whiteman AFB, Missouri. (*185th ARW*)

the change to tankers, the 185th had been cautioned that if they chose not to, that Iowa, with two fighter squadrons, would be a likely candidate for closure action. On May 16th or earlier, the list of closures would be released.

Friday the 13th was a very lucky day in May 2005. Not only did the BRAC Report not close or downsize the 185th, but it recommended that the 185th be reequipped with ten of the improved KC-135R and/or T tankers and an increase in personnel. As the major change from the original KC-135A to the KC-135E was going from the original Pratt & Whitney J-57 to the Pratt & Whitney TF-33 turbofan engines obtained from retired Boeing 707 airliners, the R model and T model were re-engined with the CFM International (General Electric and Snecma joint group built) F108 high-bypass turbofan engine. With this new engine, the R and T models had increased takeoff weight and carrying capability, improved fuel efficiency, and reduced engine noise and pollution levels. With these efficiencies, the R/T cost less to operate and maintain. Other improvements included communications, navigation, autopilot, and surveillance equipment. It was anticipated that Sioux City would get the updated KC-135s in 2006.

Disaster was in the making on August 28, 2005, as Katrina, a Category 5 hurricane, moved over the Gulf of Mexico at 175 miles per hour towards Louisiana. At 7:10 the next morning, Katrina invaded Plaquemines Parish, Louisiana, as a Category 3 hurricane, speeding along at 125 miles per hour. From Florida west to Texas, severe destruction was caused by the hurricane's resulting storm surge. The levee system around New Orleans, Louisiana, failed, bringing about major destruction and death.

Wednesday, August 31st, Iowa Governor Thomas J. Vilsack announced that he was sending nearly 100 soldiers, airmen, and health professionals to the devastated area. This was only the beginning; many more would follow. The 185th was put on alert to support Operation Katrina with four aircraft. The first mission was scheduled for Thursday, in which they were to fly generators to New Orleans for the refugees in the Superdome. Unfortunately, before this could be carried out the flooding conditions at the Superdome caused the evacuation of the Superdome and the flight was put on hold. On Friday missions were begun, with three KC-135s flying to Louis Armstrong International Airport in New Orleans, where refugees, many in wheelchairs, were flown to Kelly AFB, near San Antonio, Texas. These KC-135s carried a crew of 10 and 40 refugees each. To be self-sufficient, including security, the 10 crewmembers included three pilots, two boom operators, three crew chiefs, and two security police.

Through the month of September, a total of 78 sorties were flown, the most by any KC-135 unit. A total of 185 185th members supported Operation Katrina. They flew all over the U.S., transporting medical personnel into the disaster area, refugees out of the disaster area, and taking military police personnel to New Orleans, as well as transporting needed supplies and equipment, such as 200-kilowatt mobile power generators.

The entire area was a disaster zone, including both the airport and Naval Air Station New Orleans. Both suffered damage, and only one runway was operational at each. Arrival and departure timing had to be right on due to the heavy traffic loads at each facility.

As operations wound down in late September, the Air Guard was transporting personnel and equipment back to the states they came from. Some Army and Air Guard personnel were to leave the Gulf region September 24th, but it was delayed due to the arrival of Hurricane Rita. The 185th measured up to the Herculean effort that this humanitarian mission called for.

During the first full week of June 2006, a team from the National Guard Bureau in Washington, D.C., were at the Sioux City Air Guard base for a week of planning in preparation for conversion to the KC-135R tanker. The 2005 BRAC report recommended that Sioux City receive the R-model from Washington state Air National Guard's 141st Air Refueling Wing at Fairchild AFB. In turn, the 141st would share KC-135 aircraft with the USAF's 92nd Air Refueling Wing at that same base. At the time the BRAC report came out in 2005, it was thought, or hoped, that the conversion would start in 2006. Now it was estimated that it would not be until 2007.

January 2007 ushered in a new year and a new experience for the 185th. They would undergo their first Operational Readiness Inspection, or ORI, as an air refueling outfit. For the ORI, which would be conducted at Gulfport, Mississippi, they sent three KC-135s, five crews, and about 200 other personnel. At Gulfport, they would undergo a joint ORI with the 186th Air Refueling Wing out of Meridian, Mississippi. Starting on the 21st, the inspection lasted eight days, in which they had to fend off saboteurs, chemical and other ordnance attacks, and attacking enemy forces while remaining operational. It was very rare that a unit received an excellent grade in an ORI immediately following a conversion, but the 185th did. Colonel John Almind, team chief of the inspection team, stated afterwards, "It was obvious that the 185th ARW thoroughly prepared for this mission."

In May, it was announced that 185th Air Refueling Wing commander, Colonel John P. Janson, would be retiring, and that Lt. Col. (Col. Select) Brian A. Miller would take over command of the wing.

Satellite image of Hurricane Katrina. (NOAA)

July 9, 2007, the last KC-135E departs from Sioux City to retire in Arizona. (*185th ARW*)

Epilogue

Today's 174th Air Refueling Squadron and its parent organization, the 185th Air Refueling Wing, started taking shape in 2007.

As they did when converting to the KC-135E, they are once again depending on the 141st Air Refueling Wing of the Washington State Air Guard to help in pilot and maintenance training and receiving their new aircraft from them; in this case KC-135Rs and some Ts. The first KC-135R arrived July 9th, with Sioux City pilot Lt. Col. Kurt Kindschuh as aircraft commander. Col. Kindschuh and his crew had trained for two weeks, in which they flew a flight simulator three times and the actual aircraft three times. Now they would pass their knowledge to other Sioux City guardsmen. By early August, they would have their second tanker.

Change of aircraft was not the only change for the 185th. On the morning of August 4, 2007, Lt. Col. Brian A. Miller became the wing's new commander in a Change-of-Command ceremony. With a 31-year military career, and 185th commander for five years and ten months, USAF Academy graduate Col. John P. Janson retired.

Aircraft deployments were not the only deployments for the Sioux City unit. Civil engineering, security forces, and others deployed on numerous missions in their specialties over the years. In August 2007, the unit had a number of personnel in areas along the Mexican border as part of Operation Jump Start. This was a joint operation between the National Guard and the U.S. Department of Homeland Security and the U.S. Customs and Border Protection agencies in securing that border.

As do all National Guard units, Air and Army, the 185th has both the federal and the state side of their responsibilities. More often than not, the state side, as do some federal, operations involve natural disasters. In early June 2008, Iowa experienced massive flooding along the Mississippi River on its eastern side. Flooding was experienced from a number of rivers, including the Cedar River. The disaster lasted into early July. Over 500 members of the 185th aided in the search and rescue effort.

With the KC-135R tanker's greater fuel efficient engines, longer range, and greater load carrying capability, the 174th Air Refueling Squadron was in a position to provide tanker support world-wide. In late April 2008, they sent aircraft and about 150 personnel to Manas AB (sometimes referred to as Ganci AB), Kyrgyzstan. There the Total Force concept is in full operation and working very well.

At Manas AB is the 376th Air Expeditionary Wing, which is a composite active duty Air

"The Veteran" was the last KC-135E at Sioux City. Its nose art depicts the Vietnam memorial in honor of those that served during that war, including the 174th Tactical Fighter Squadron. (*185th ARW*)

Force, Air Force Reserve, and with the arrival of the 174th tankers with support members from the 185th, Air National Guard. The 376th is known as the Liberandos, a nickname used by the 376th Bombardment Group in World War II. They were part of the raid on Ploesti, Romania. They also made the news in 1958, when the remains of one of their World War II B-24 Liberators, "Lady Be Good," was discovered in the Libyan desert.

Due to the mountainous terrain of Afghanistan, the crews found the missions challenging. Their mission was to provide fuel to the aircraft supporting the ground forces in Afghanistan as part of Operation Enduring Freedom. The Sioux City troops set a number of records while flying out of Manas. They set several fuel offload records while fueling tactical aircraft over Afghanistan. They never missed a sortie due to either maintenance or weather, and they achieved the highest Mission Ready rate that Manas AB had ever experienced to that time.

Both the country and the people of Afghanistan could be called rugged. This was found out when the Soviet Union invaded Afghanistan in 1979, and after nine years gave up and left. Afghanistan is a very poor country, with a central government that is quite corrupt. A great majority of its people have no electricity, running water, or sanitary facilities for bodily functions. Apparently, a segment of the population does not know that they are part of the country of Afghanistan; it's the tribe, the tribal leaders, and religious leaders that interpret the law from the Koran. Their only source of news, or information, is from those leaders. It is a daunting task that the American forces and their allies have undertaken, and the National Guard, Air and Army, have performed wholeheartedly.

One of the 185th ARW's KC-135Rs serving as part of the 376th Air Expeditionary Wing at Manas AB, Kyrgyzstan. (*185th ARW*)

For the Sioux City guardsmen, the pace was quick and the length of their missions long. They flew 288 combat sorties, accounting for 1,451 flight hours. They offloaded 15.8 million pounds of fuel to 621 receiver aircraft. Col. Randy Ogden, 376th Expeditionary Operations Group commander, a reservist, stated: "You go on an airplane, you can't tell which crew chief is active duty or which one is Guard." That's quite an endorsement. One of the differences in the support personnel was that the guard members could have over 20 years' experience and be in their forties, while the active duty troop might be in his early twenties with a year or two of experience. Both the guardsman and active duty airmen found that they could learn from each other, and both go home with a positive experience to share with others.

The 185th Air Refueling Wing had taken preemptive action to insure their ability to integrate with the active duty Air Force at Manas AB. The Air Force KC-135Rs incorporated the Block 40 upgrade, which dealt with radios and navigation systems. The Air Guard KC-135s were of the Block 30 configuration. Though the 174th's tankers would not start the upgrade process until late 2009, the wing's commander, Col. Brian Miller, directed that the pilots and boom operators receive training for Block 40 upgrades, so they could be more fully integrated at Manas. This was a cooperative effort, as the Air Guard at Fairchild AFB, Washington, assisted in training and provided simulator time.

The tanker's primary mission is refueling. In the Iraq and Afghanistan war zone, the aircraft refueled by the 174th could be of any U.S. service or allied nation. And that is not all they do. They hauled personnel and pallets of supplies wherever they were needed. From the war zone they evacuated the wounded to hospitals in Germany, the U.S., or wherever. As has always been the case with the 174th and its parent 185th, there is always humanitarian work, be it an orphanage, leprosy hospital, or whatever the local need happens to be.

On this support mission over Afghanistan, the 174th services an F-15E Strike Eagle. (*185th ARW*)

Their deployments were quite unlike those of their fighter days. The best example of "the old days" was the 174th's deployment to Vietnam in 1968. Here 22 F-100C fighters, hundreds of personnel, and thousands of pounds of equipment and supplies deployed for a year. They had a large crowd sending them off, and not only another large welcoming crowd when they returned, but Sioux City gave them a parade. The tanker world is quite different. Quite often it is one aircraft and the aircrew, maybe two for relief. And with the Iraq and Afghan turmoil they are constantly on these missions of one or two aircraft. But being highly trained professionals, the entire 185th Air Refueling Wing takes great pride, deserved pride, in their work.

The 174th Air Refueling Squadron received its eighth KC-135R in July 2009. The conversion effort was complete. This one was quite a bit easier than going from jet fighters to tankers. This time most of the cost, around $1 million, was for training.

Between mid-August and early September 2009, the 174th took part in an exercise called Badger Denial. Because combat flying operations are generally at lower altitudes than the Military Operating Areas across the U.S., airspace was cleared for this exercise over a large part of the northwest quadrant of Iowa. The 174th's KC-135s fueled F-16s from Des Moines between the Iowa cities of Spencer and Estherville. The aerial

One of Sioux City's KC-135Rs refuels a B-1B from Ellsworth AFB, South Dakota, over Afghanistan while serving in the 376th Air Expeditionary Wing. (*185th ARW*)

refueling took place around 20,000 feet. The fighters operated between 10,000 and 18,000 feet, and lower at times. The public was warned that there could be a good bit of air activity at night, some involving flares. Army National Guard were maneuvering throughout the area in a variety of military vehicles.

In December 2009, the 174th sent their first KC-135R to Kelly AFB in San Antonio, Texas, where Rockwell International incorporated Block 40 changes. The KC-135Rs of the 174th are of Block 30 configuration. It took about 35 days to incorporate changes to the communications and navigation systems. The upgrades included improved communications that enable the pilots to better communicate with active duty U.S. and allied air forces, and improved maintenance diagnostics. Both pilots and maintenance personnel started training for the upgrade in 2008. The first upgraded KC-135 was received by the 174th in January 2010.

A major deployment event for the Sioux City Air Guard was 185th commanding officer Col. Brian A. Miller being deployed to International Security Assistance Force (ISAF) Headquarters in Kabul, Afghanistan, in August 2010. There Col. Miller served as the Vice Commander of the 9th Air and Space Expeditionary Task Force, Afghanistan, and as Deputy Director Air Component Coordination Element, Afghanistan. In that position, Col. Miller advised the Commander of ISAF and his Senior Joint Coalition staff on air power matters, as well as performing the duties as Vice Commander. The 9th had over 8,500 airmen in Afghanistan. His assignment was well timed. The buildup of troops and equipment started in 2009, as U.S. forces moved out of Iraq. When Col. Miller arrived in Afghanistan, the pace was reaching a peak in increased activity. Miller returned to Sioux City in April 2011. During his absence Col. Edward A. Sauley III was interim commander of the 185th.

Personnel of the 185th ARW arriving at Manas AB to serve as part of the 376th Air Expeditionary Wing "Liberandos'" "Tanker Total Force." (*185th ARW*)

185th's Col. Brian A. Miller. (*185th ARW*)

174th ARS KC-135R at Williamtown Royal Australian Air Force Base in Australia. The 174th supported RAAF F/A-18s and Iowa ANG 124th FS from Des Moines in the Dissimilar Air Combat Training in operation Sentry Down Under in 2011. (*132nd FW*)

Lt. Col. Kurt Kindschuh of the 185th ARW flying one of the Sioux City tankers during Sentry Down Under. (*132nd FW*)

Mission down under was an all-Iowa experience. The Royal Australian Air Force holds a semi-annual exercise called Sentry Down Under. Iowa's two flying squadrons, the 124th Fighter Squadron (132nd Fighter Wing) out of Des Moines and the 174th Air Refueling Squadron (185th Air Refueling Wing) out of Sioux City, were invited to participate in the early-2011 exercise. For the 124th Fighter Squadron, this would be Dissimilar Air Combat Training, as their F-16s flew mock combat against Royal Australian Air Force F/A-18s.

For the 174th Air Refueling Squadron, it was training all the way. The 174th aided in hauling some of the 124th Fighter Squadron's 88 tons of equipment and 125 personnel; a C-5 and C-17 did most of the hauling. The 174th also provided fuel for the 124th's eight F-16s, both going to and returning from Australia. The 174th provided one KC-135 and 21 personnel for this three-week effort.

The USAF uses the flying boom system for refueling their aircraft. This system was designed by Boeing. Most foreign countries and the U.S. Navy use the probe and drogue system, which was initially developed by the British during World War II. The 174th boom operators have very little experience in probe and drogue operations, so this was a good experience for them, as their flying boom can be adapted to this system. In the flying boom system, the aircraft to receive fuel flies up to a set point from the tanker, and then the boom operator maneuvers the tip of the boom into the fuel receptacle of the

A pair of Royal Australian Air Force F/A-18s approach a 174th KC-135R for fuel. (*185th ARW*)

174th ARS boom operator MSgt David Dietrich reviewing his checklist in preparation for refueling one of the 124th FS's F-16s during Sentry Down Under exercises. (*132nd FW*)

receiving aircraft. In the probe and drogue system, the boom operator extends the drogue and the receiving aircraft has to do the maneuvering to get its probe into the drogue (this is not considered x-rated action).

Al-Thawrat, al-Arabiyyah, or commonly translated, Arab Spring. This turmoil started in the Arab world in December 2010, when the Tunisian President, Zine El Abidine Ben Ali, was deposed. On February 15th of the following year, anti-government protests began in Libya. Because of Colonel Moammar Gadhafi's bloody attacks on his own people, the United Nations Security Council adapted Resolution 1973 on March 17, 2011, which authorized a no-fly zone, and stated that all necessary measures were to be taken to protect Libyan civilians. On the 19th, a coalition of the U.S., the United Kingdom, and France intervened with a bombing campaign against Libyan government forces. U.S.-directed actions were carried out under Operation Odyssey Dawn.

To support the coalition air operations, aerial refueling tankers were necessary. Where to get the tankers was quickly decided upon—the Air National Guard and Air Force Reserve. Calls were immediately made to the Guard and Reserve bases, where within 36 hours tankers (KC-135s and KC-10s) from 50 different locations were all on their way to the 313th Air Expeditionary Wing, which

U.S. Air Force F-16s awaiting their turn to be refueled from a 174th ARS KC-135. (*185th ARW*)

An example of multi-point refueling. In this method, up to three aircraft using the "probe and drogue" technique can be refueled. (931st ARG)

The "flying boom," developed by Boeing and part of the KC-135 series aircraft, is the method used by the USAF. The U.S. Navy and most foreign countries use the "probe and drogue" system. The boom on the KC-135 can be adapted to accommodate the "probe and drogue" method of aerial refueling. (*185th ARW*)

was just being formed at Moron AB, Spain. All of these reserve forces were volunteers. To command this wing, Brig. Gen. Roy E. Uptegraff III, commander of Pennsylvania Air National Guard's 171st Air Refueling Wing, was picked. On March 18th, he received a phone call in which he was asked if he would deploy to an undisclosed location as part of the initial support for Operation Odyssey Dawn. The following day he had consultations with Col. Richard J. Evans III, commander of Nebraska's 155 Air Refueling Wing, Air Mobility Command at Scott AFB, Illinois, the 18th Air Force, also at Scott AFB, and his own staff. The next day, General Uptegraff was finalizing plans with his staff as to personnel and equipment to be taken when he received another call; this time it was to deploy. By 10 o'clock that evening he and his team were airborne.

It was announced on March 28th that 11 Air National Guard tanker wings had been enlisted to support Odyssey Dawn. They were from Arizona, Arkansas, Illinois, Iowa, Michigan, Nebraska, New Jersey, Ohio, Pennsylvania, Tennessee, and Utah. Their mission was to refuel the coalition warfighters that were taking out Libya's integrated air and missile defense systems and other military facilities. By the end of March, all operations in response to United Nations resolutions 1970 and 1973 were under the North Atlantic Treaty Organization's (NATO) control, and the operation was called Unified Protector.

Once again, the importance of the Air Guard had a spotlight on it. Air Force Lt. Gen. Harry M. Wyatt III stated: "The Air Guard has the experience and expertise to mobilize quickly, deploy and integrate with any joint or coalition effort anywhere in the world." When the Air Force realized the great need for aerial refueling, they contacted each wing directly. Early on March 26th, all eleven Air Guard wings sent aircraft, crews, and maintainers to Moron AB, where they formed the 313th Air Expeditionary Wing. The 313th was made up of both Air National Guard and Air Force Reserve KC-135 and KC-10 tankers, as well as USAF personnel.

Initially, the duration of their deployment was unknown. Eventually rotation of personnel started at about the 90-day mark. Most USAF aircraft utilize the flying boom system, but the U.S. Navy and other nations use the probe and drogue system. The KC-135Rs of the 174th Air Refueling Squadron, and of other units, can use a single point attachment to the boom, or through a pod under the wing use the

Operation Odyssey Dawn/Unified Protector was staged out of Moron AB, Spain. Brig. Gen. Roy E. Uptegraff, on the left, was the original commander of the 313th Air Expeditionary Wing. Taking over the 313th in June 2011 was Col. Ted Metzgar (right). (128th ARW)

A 174th ARS crew has completed their day with the 313th Air Expeditionary Wing in Spain. (*185th ARW*)

multipoint refueling system, in which two aircraft can be refueled at once. The boom operators of the Guard and Reserve were more familiar with the boom, but quickly were at ease and very capable in supporting the coalition aircraft that were not capable of using the boom.

In T. S. Eliot's "Old Possum's Book of Practical Cats," as was in the stage play and movie "CATS," we have Mungojerrie and Rumpelteazer, which are, according to Eliot, "a very notorious couple of cats." One day General Uptegraff was on the ramp at Moron AB and viewed the tankers from many units, remarking that they looked like "calico cats." It wasn't that they were notorious, but like Mungojerrie and Rumpelteazer, two calico cats, they were colorful. Each of the Air National Guard and Air Force Reserve tankers had its own unique tail flashes; thus, the Calico Wing came about.

Libyan rebel leaders declared Libya liberated October 23, 2011. Operation Unified Protector ended October 31, 2011. Col. Ted Metzgar, commander of Wisconsin's 128th Air Refueling Wing, became commander of the 313th Air Expeditionary Wing June 17, 2011. The 313th had consisted of over 800 personnel from the active Air Force, Guard, and Reserve, and more than 25 tankers. They flew more than 2,200 sorties and nearly 20,000 flight hours. The 174th Air Refueling Squadron aircrews flew 58 sorties, 516 flight hours, and offloaded 1,700,000 pounds of fuel while maintaining a 98 percent readiness rate.

The 313th was the poster child for Total Force. A good example was on May 22nd, when the crew of aircraft commander Capt. Jeff Lascurain, 1st Lt. Spencer Liedl, pilot, and Tech. Sgt. Christopher Slater, boom operator, flew the 313th's 1,000th sortie. Lascurain and Liedl were active Air Force and Slater was from the Illinois Air Guard. To add to the team, the crew chiefs that helped recover the KC-135, Tech. Sgt. Andrew Nelson and Staff Sgt. Matthew Jackson, were guardsmen from Bangor, Maine, along with Senior Airman Stephen Vanderhorst of the Ohio Air Guard. Though it was not stated who the aircraft belonged to, in a similar case, with a mix of Air Force and Air National Guard personnel, the KC-135 used was of the Air Force Reserve.

While the Air Guardsmen of Sioux City were in Spain supporting Operation Odyssey Dawn/ Unified Protector, the guardsmen left behind were not idle. In June 2011, due to high water release by the U.S. Army Corps of Engineers, flooding started along the Missouri River from South Dakota south. The flooding in the Missouri River caused flooding in its tributaries, including the Big Sioux River. 185th Air Refueling Wing guardsmen patrolled the levees along the Big Sioux River, ensuring that there were no breaks in the levee system caused by nature or intruding humans. The flooding decreased below flood stage in September, but millions, if not billions, of dollars of damage was sustained, farm lands were adversely impacted, and thousands of

The business end for the tankers in support of Operation Unified Protector. A Royal Netherlands Air Force F-16AN receives fuel from a 174th ARS KC-135. (*185th ARW*)

313th Air Expeditionary Wing—The Calico Wing. (*185th ARW*)

Air and Army National Guard members were both assigned and volunteered to battle the Iowa floods of 2008. (*185th ARW*)

Thousands of sandbags meant many hours of hard work. (*185th ARW*)

trees were killed by the water surrounding them for an extended period.

Another joint operation, Badger Denial, where the 174th provided the air refueling, began on August 9th and, over selected days, ran into December. The operating area for the ground and air contingents was over a good part of northwest Iowa, with the 174th operating between the towns of Spencer and Estherville. The Air Guard notified the public that "at no time will anything be dropped from aircraft,..." This was a joint active duty and reserve forces exercise, both air and ground.

Once again, the 185th Air Refueling wing deployed aircraft and support personnel to Geilenkirchen AB, Germany, to support NATO's E-3 Sentry operations. In July 2011, two KC-135s and over 40 personnel were sent for the seventh time to provide the multi-national NATO pilots with air-to-air refueling, training the Air Guard tanker crews in working with other nations in the NATO environment. Later on, another KC-135 plus support personnel was sent to Forward Operating Base at Aktion, Greece. At this time, Lt. Col. David McKinney, 185th Vice Commander, was completing his four year tour as Air National Guard Liaison at Geilenkirchen AB.

The 185th Air Refueling Wing had put out a great effort during 2011. It was not only the flying operations of the 174th Air Refueling Squadron, but the wing's security force, civil engineering, and the unit's participation in the agribusiness development team. In November, the 185th was

A 174th ARS KC-135 on duty in Europe refuels a NATO E-3A AWACS aircraft over the North Sea. (*185th ARW*)

presented the 2011 Major General Stanley F. H. Newman Outstanding Unit Award by the Airlift/Tanker Association in Nashville, Tennessee. This award is given to the unit that "...embodies the spirit and essence of the Citizen Airman balancing the operational demands of today's global mobility operations, maintaining a viable strategic reserve for tomorrow while embracing responsibilities to their civilian employer, community, and family."

As 2012 opened, the 185th was a recognized unit of excellence. Their record for the previous year had the statistics to prove it. They had over 300 members deployed to numerous locations around the world. Their deployments equated to over 20,000 man-days. They had just received a prestigious award from the Airlift/Tanker Association as an Outstanding Unit. Their fleet had also grown to nine KC-135Rs, which enabled them to provide even greater service to military aviation all over the world. The awards continued to come to the 185th. On January 25, 2012, it was announced that they had been awarded the Air Force Outstanding Unit Award for achievements from November 2009 to October 2011.

Over the years, the 185th held off-site meetings to accomplish mandatory annual training and to discuss expectations for the upcoming year. A major item of interest in the January 2012 meeting was the upcoming Department of Defense budget. The 185th realized the reduced budget could have an effect, but believed that due to readiness for mobility, great performance record, and being recognized as an elite unit, they were in a good position to weather whatever happened.

The bad news came down in early February; the Air Force announced that its Fiscal Year 2013 Total Force Manpower Force Structure impacted both of Iowa's Air National Guard wings. In the budget cutting, the 185th would go from 9 KC-135Rs

Air National Guard director, Gen. Harry M. Wyatt III, presents 185th ARW commander Col. Brian A. Miller the Airlift/Tanker Association's 2011 Maj. Gen. Stanley F. H. Newman Air National Guard Outstanding Unit Award in Nashville, Tennessee, November 5, 2011. (*185th ARW*)

to eight, but would have a net increase of three personnel. The 132nd Fighter Wing would be greatly impacted. The Air Force recommended eliminating their 21 F-16s altogether, and reduced their manning by almost 500 personnel. The 132nd would become a drone unit.

On March 6th, the Air Force submitted their plan to Congress. Local and state leaders had started a campaign in early February to convince first the Air Force and then Congress that the 185th proved its worth as an elite unit, and was valuable to Air Force operations world-wide, and the cost to the Air Force for the Air Guard was less than active duty units. The fight was going on as of the end of April.

How history seems to repeat itself. The U.S. Army Air Forces were against having an Air National Guard when the War Department was planning for one during World War II. In the 1950s and 1960s, there were a number of efforts to eliminate the Air Guard, or combine it with the Reserves. It also seems that the Air Guard is easily sacrificed during times of budget cuts. In the 1950s, there was some rationale for such actions. The guard greatly improved in the 1960s, to the point where they were no longer second rate. The 174th Tactical Fighter Squadron was a key player in showing that the Air Guard was as good, and at times better, in capability, maintainability, and *esprit de corps*. In Vietnam, they bombed as good if not better than the regulars. Their maintenance personnel performed above all the rest and showed in the squadron's in-commission rate. And since the 1970s, to date, the 174th Squadron, as well as the entire 185th, showed that they could be mobilized at a moment's notice, quickly deploy to a distant land, and begin operating almost immediately.

At this present time, and into the future, the Sioux City Air Guard will accomplish whatever mission comes their way. If you think they are an elite unit now, watch them improve even further. They will never sit back and wait. They will step up and ahead of all the rest. There are many more "missions accomplished" coming their way, and they will receive many more "outstanding" awards. The twenty-first century has just begun.

Appendices

Appendix A
Lineage

April 27,1943 Constituted 386th Fighter Squadron
May 15, 1943 Activated
September 22, 1945 Inactivated
May 24, 1946 Redesignated 174th Fighter Squadron, Single Engine and allotted to Air National Guard
December 2, 1946 176 Fighter Squadron, SE Federally Recognized
May 1, 1950 Redesignated 174th Fighter Squadron, Jet
June 1, 1951 Redesignated 174th Fighter-Bomber Squadron
July 1, 1955 Redesignated 174th Fighter-Interceptor Squadron
April 10, 1958 Redesignated 174th Tactical Reconnaissance Squadron
May 1, 1961 (some sources state Feb 5, 1961) Redesignated 174th Tactical Fighter Squadron (Special Delivery); SD dropped at some unknown time
March 16, 1992 Redesignated 174th Fighter Squadron
June 1, 2003 Redesignated 174th Air Refueling Squadron

Appendix B
Aircraft
(estimated dates squadron was operational with these aircraft)
P-51D* February 1947 – April 1950
F-84B April 1950 – last half 1951
F-51D last half 1951 – December 1952
F-51D April 1953 – July 1953
F-80A and F-80B** August 1953 – May 1956
F-84E June 1956 – May 1958
RF-84F and RF-84K May 1958 – August 1961
F-84F May 1958 – December 1958
F-100C and F-100F July 1961 – March 1974
F-100D and F-100F March 1974 – March 1977
A-7D and A-7K April 1977 – January 1992
F-16C and F-16D April 1992 – December 2002
KC-135E April 2004 – October 2007
KC-135R and KC-135T October 2007 – Present

* In June 1948, the Air Force changed their designation system, and P for pursuit changed to F for fighter (P-51D became F-51D).

** Most of these aircraft were sent to Lockheed in California for upgrading and redesignated F-80C-11 and F-80C-12.

Appendix C
174th Squadron Commanders

Lt. Col. Morgan R. Harrison	December 2, 1946
Maj. J. Allen Orr	September 1, 1947
Maj. Robert C. Ruby	August 14, 1948
Maj. Rollin M. Batten, jr.	January 7, 1952
Unknown Acting C.O.	January 1, 1953
Capt. Donald W. Forney	January 28, 1953
Maj. Warren G. "Bud" Nelson	October 1, 1962
Maj. Gordon L. Young	1968 - 1969
Lt. Col Dudley P. Smidt	1973
Lt. Col. Patrick C. Parks	1980
Lt. Col. Sherman H. Sawin	1981 – 1983
Lt. Col. John O. Ahnert jr.	1984 – 1986
Lt. Col. Bill Hagemeyer	1987 – 1989
Unknown	1990 - 1995
Lt. Col. David E. Lundquist	1996
Unknown	1997 - 2004
Lt. Col. Brian A. Miller	May 2004
Unknown	Feb. 2005
Unknown	2006 - 2009
Lt. Col. Chet P. Hahn	2010
Lt. Col. James E. Walker	2011
Col. Edward A. Sauley III	2012

Appendices

Appendix A
Lineage

April 27,1943 Constituted 386th Fighter Squadron
May 15, 1943 Activated
September 22, 1945 Inactivated
May 24, 1946 Redesignated 174th Fighter Squadron, Single Engine and allotted to Air National Guard
December 2, 1946 176 Fighter Squadron, SE Federally Recognized
May 1, 1950 Redesignated 174th Fighter Squadron, Jet
June 1, 1951 Redesignated 174th Fighter-Bomber Squadron
July 1, 1955 Redesignated 174th Fighter-Interceptor Squadron
April 10, 1958 Redesignated 174th Tactical Reconnaissance Squadron
May 1, 1961 (some sources state Feb 5, 1961) Redesignated 174th Tactical Fighter Squadron (Special Delivery); SD dropped at some unknown time
March 16, 1992 Redesignated 174th Fighter Squadron
June 1, 2003 Redesignated 174th Air Refueling Squadron

Appendix B
Aircraft

(estimated dates squadron was operational with these aircraft)
P-51D* February 1947 – April 1950
F-84B April 1950 – last half 1951
F-51D last half 1951 – December 1952
F-51D April 1953 – July 1953
F-80A and F-80B** August 1953 – May 1956
F-84E June 1956 – May 1958
RF-84F and RF-84K May 1958 – August 1961
F-84F May 1958 – December 1958
F-100C and F-100F July 1961 – March 1974
F-100D and F-100F March 1974 – March 1977
A-7D and A-7K April 1977 – January 1992
F-16C and F-16D April 1992 – December 2002
KC-135E April 2004 – October 2007
KC-135R and KC-135T October 2007 – Present

* In June 1948, the Air Force changed their designation system, and P for pursuit changed to F for fighter (P-51D became F-51D).

** Most of these aircraft were sent to Lockheed in California for upgrading and redesignated F-80C-11 and F-80C-12.

Appendix C
174th Squadron Commanders

Lt. Col. Morgan R. Harrison	December 2, 1946
Maj. J. Allen Orr	September 1, 1947
Maj. Robert C. Ruby	August 14, 1948
Maj. Rollin M. Batten, jr.	January 7, 1952
Unknown Acting C.O.	January 1, 1953
Capt. Donald W. Forney	January 28, 1953
Maj. Warren G. "Bud" Nelson	October 1, 1962
Maj. Gordon L. Young	1968 - 1964
Lt. Col Dudley P. Smidt	1972
Lt. Col. Patrick C. Parks	1976
Lt. Col. Sherman H. Swain	1981
Lt. Col. John O. Ahnert jr.	1983
Lt. Col. Bill Hagemeyer	October 1987
Lt. Col. William W. Hagemeyer	Oct. 1987
Lt. Col. Leslie C. Jensen	June 1990
Lt. Col. Allen J. Smith	October 1991
Lt. Col. Dwayne A. Alons	August 1992
Lt. Col. Timothy J. Goldhammer	April 1994
Lt. Col. David E. Lundquist	July 1994
Lt. Col. David F. Crowden	1997
Lt. Col. Rodney I. Spahn	January 8, 2000
Lt. Col. Glenn Messner	November 11, 2002
Lt. Col. Brian A. Miller	May 2004
Unknown	February 2005
Unknown	2006 - 2007
Lt. Col. David McKinney	2008
Lt. Col. Chet P. Hahn	2010
Lt. Col. James E. Walker	2011
Col. Edward A. Sauley III	2012
Lt. Col. Kevin Slaughter	Jun. 2013

Appendix D Squadron Emblems

174TH FIGHTER-BOMBER SQUADRON

The 174th's first official emblem approved March 24, 1954. The unit was a fighter-bomber squadron at the time. (*174th FBS/ McCallum collection*)

The second emblem was a modification of the first. It depicted the squadron in the reconnaissance role. Approved August 3, 1959. (*174th TRS/McCallum collection*)

The third was a major revision of the Indian chieftain theme. This version was approved May 13, 1971. To the present day, this has remained the basic squadron emblem; only the squadron designation has been updated over time. (*174th TFS/McCallum collection*)

Two versions of the 174th Fighter Squadron version of the above emblem. (*174th FS/ McCallum collection*) and (Air *National Guard Bureau/History Office* website)

174th Air Refueling Squadron of today. (*185th ARW website*)

Appendix G Deployment Route

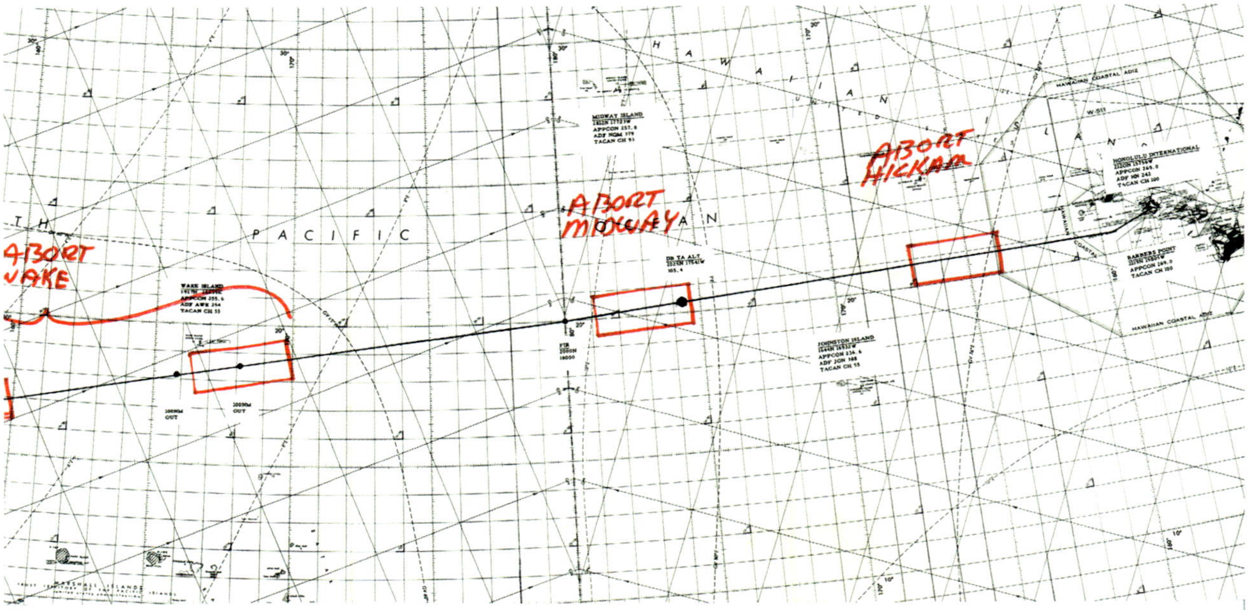

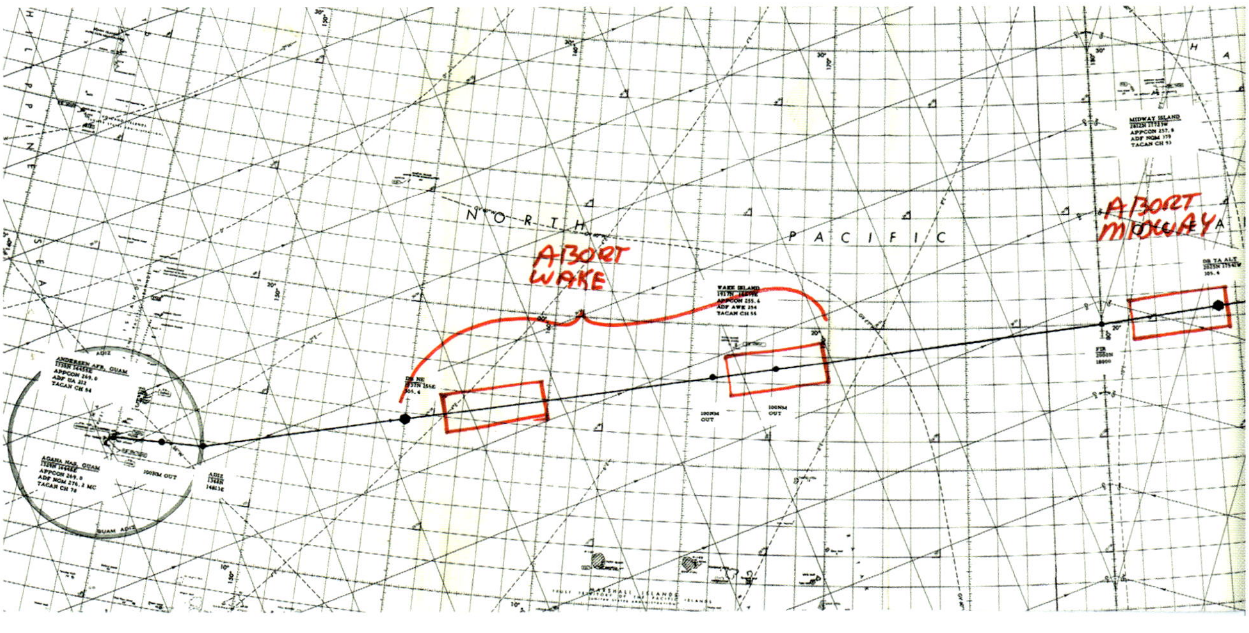

Deployment route from Vietnam Deployment Book. (*Darrell E. Lake*)

Appendix H Tanker/Receiver Aircraft Line-up Sheet

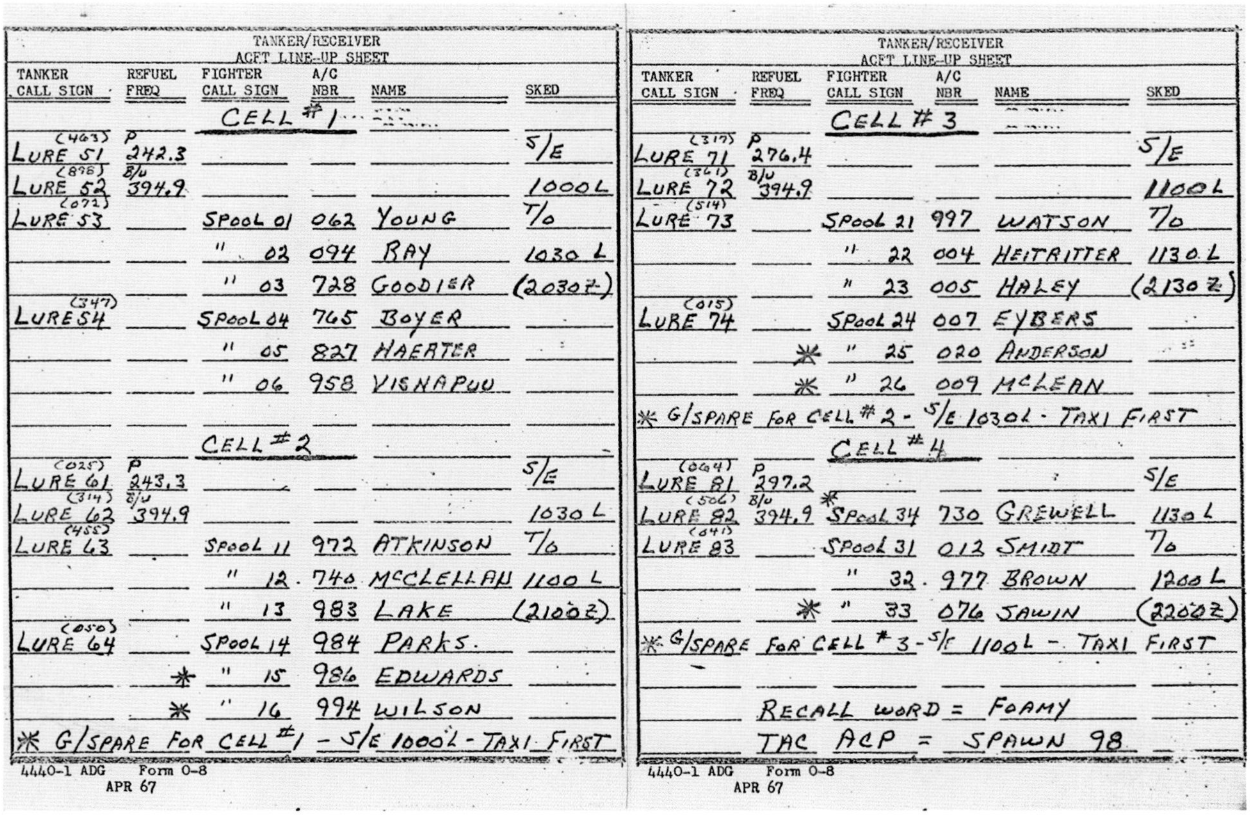

TANKER/RECEIVER
ACFT LINE-UP SHEET

TANKER CALL SIGN	REFUEL FREQ	FIGHTER CALL SIGN	A/C NBR	NAME	SKED
		CELL #1			
(463) LURE 51	P 242.3				S/E
(898) LURE 52	B/U 394.9				1000L
(072) LURE 53		SPOOL 01	062	YOUNG	T/O
		" 02	094	RAY	1030 L
		" 03	728	GOODIER	(2030Z)
(347) LURE 54		SPOOL 04	765	BOYER	
		" 05	827	HAERTER	
		" 06	958	VISNAPUU	
		CELL #2			
(025) LURE 61	P 243.3				S/E
(314) LURE 62	B/U 394.9				1030 L
(455) LURE 63		SPOOL 11	972	ATKINSON	T/O
		" 12	740	McCLELLAN	1100 L
		" 13	983	LAKE	(2100Z)
(050) LURE 64		SPOOL 14	984	PARKS.	
	*	" 15	986	EDWARDS	
	*	" 16	994	WILSON	
* G/SPARE FOR CELL #1 - S/E 1000L - TAXI FIRST					

4440-1 ADG Form 0-8
APR 67

TANKER/RECEIVER
ACFT LINE-UP SHEET

TANKER CALL SIGN	REFUEL FREQ	FIGHTER CALL SIGN	A/C NBR	NAME	SKED
		CELL #3			
(317) LURE 71	P 276.4				S/E
(361) LURE 72	B/U 394.9				1100L
(514) LURE 73		SPOOL 21	997	WATSON	T/O
		" 22	004	HEITRITTER	1130 L
		" 23	005	HALEY	(2130Z)
(015) LURE 74		SPOOL 24	007	EYBERS	
	*	" 25	020	ANDERSON	
	*	" 26	009	McLEAN	
* G/SPARE FOR CELL #2 - S/E 1030L - TAXI FIRST					
		CELL #4			
(064) LURE 81	P 297.2				S/E
(506) LURE 82	B/U 394.9	* SPOOL 34	730	GREWELL	1130 L
(041) LURE 83		SPOOL 31	012	SMIDT	T/O
		" 32	977	BROWN	1200 L
	*	" 33	076	SAWIN	(2200Z)
* G/SPARE FOR CELL #3 - S/E 1100L - TAXI FIRST					
		RECALL WORD = FOAMY			
		TAC ACP = SPAWN 98			

4440-1 ADG Form 0-8
APR 67

Tanker/Receiver Aircraft Line-up Sheet from Vietnam Deployment Book.
(*Darrell E. Lake*)

Appendix I Vietman F-100C Nose Art

NO HAND HOLD
HOWIE

HOMBRE

CAPT. ANDY ANDERSON
300 lbs
Ballast
Installed
020

F-100C Vietnam nose art taken shortly after their return to Sioux City. (*185th TFG/McCallum collection*)

Bibliography of Major Works

Francillon, Rene J. *The Untied States Air National Guard.* Westport, CT: Airtime Publishing, 1993

Gross, Charles J., Dr. *A Chronological History of the Air National Guard and Its Antecedents, 1908-2007*, www.ang.af.mil/shared/media/document/AFD-081003-052.pdf

Gross, Charles Joseph. *Prelude to the Total Force: The Air National Guard 1943-1969.* Office of Air Force History, 1985

Morrison, Robert, 1LT, ed. *185th Tactical Fighter Group, Iowa Air National Guard, 40 Years of Service to State & Country, 1946-1986.* Sioux City, 185th TFG, 1986

Morrison, Robert L., Sr., Major, ed. *The 185th Fighter Wing, Iowa Air National Guard; "The Bats," 50 Year History, 1946-1996.* Sioux City, 185th FW, 1996

Morrison, Robert, Lt. Col., ed, 185th Air Refueling Wing. "The Bats," 1946-2007, Sioux City, 185th ARW, 2007

Pellegreno, Ann Holtgren. *Iowa Takes to the Air, Volume Three 1941-2003.* Sioux City, Aerodrome Press, 2003

Index